IT'S A JUNGLE OUT THERE

THE FEMINIST SURVIVAL GUIDE TO POLITICALLY INHOSPITABLE ENVIRONMENTS

AMANDA MARCOTTE

SEAL PRESS

It's A Jungle Out There

The Feminist Survival Guide to Politically Inhospitable Environments

Copyright © 2007 Amanda Marcotte

Published by Seal Press
A Member of Perseus Books Group
1700 Fourth Street
Berkeley, CA 94710

Library of Congress Cataloging-in-Publication Data
Marcotte, Amanda.
   It's a jungle out there : the feminist survival guide to politically inhospitable environments / by Amanda Marcotte.
      p. cm.
   ISBN-13: 978-1-58005-226-9
   ISBN-10: 1-58005-226-6
1. Feminism—Humor. 2. Women—Humor. I. Title.
PN6231.F44M37 2008
818'.602—dc22

                          2007039420

Cover design by Kate Basart
Interior design by Tabitha Lahr and Sean Bellows
Cover and interior illustrations LORNA, THE JUNGLE GIRL: TM & © 2008 Marvel Characters, Inc.
Used with permission.
Printed in the U.S.A.

To Molly Ivins and all the other kick-ass feminists who've shown me that the key to surviving is laughing.

Contents

PART 3. SURVIVING THE SEXUAL MINEFIELD

PART 4. THE UGLIEST SIDE OF THE BACKLASH: FUNDAMENTALISTS AND ANTICHOICERS

PART 5. YOU DON'T NEED GOD TO TELL YOU TO BE SEXIST

PART 6. POSTFEMINISM MY ASS

PART 7. IT'S NOT A POST-FEMINIST WORLD WHEN WE HAVE A LONG WAY TO GO

PART 8. RESOURCES: HAVING FUN WHILE SURVIVING

Introduction

When a group of feminists gets together and starts talking feminism, the laws of probability decree that the question "Why don't more women, at least young women, call themselves feminists?" will arise within the space of an hour. As a central concern, it's been blown completely out of proportion, but it comes up enough that it's as good a starting point as any with which to begin this book. So, why don't more women self-identify as feminists, even though said women will invariably agree with self-proclaimed feminists that (a) men are no better than us and (b) sexism really sucks?

There are many explanations, but I think for a good majority of feminists-who-won't-use-the-word, the main motivation is fear. They're afraid of the consequences of calling themselves feminists and try to weasel out of it by denying the label.

This is the point where tradition mandates that I point out that all we have to fear is fear itself, etc., but I'm going to break with tradition, a habit of mine that led me to feminism in the first place. If you're afraid of being a feminist, it's for a good reason. It's hard to be a feminist much of the time. People are mean to feminists. They denounce you as Nazis on talk radio, bitch about you in bars, blame you for all the world's ills in conservative magazines, and call you "cunts" on Internet message boards. If you're straight, you're going to have to wade through many a date with men who look hurt that you'd dare embrace such a pro-equality political ideology. If you're a lesbian, you don't need me telling you that people can be mean. You'll have to suffer from people assuming you hate men, you hate sex, and you hate razors. Which is why this book is a survival guide, not a pep rally. It's hard out there for a feminist, though I'd always argue it's more rewarding than the alternative.

Why are people so mean to feminists? Because so much of feminism is the fine art of calling bullshit, and calling bullshit makes people uncomfortable. The first rule of understanding bullshit is to understand that people really love their bullshit. Think about the expression on your average person's face when she's contemplating her favorite bit of bullshit—the slack jaw, the vague smile, the vacant light in her eyes indicating that whoever was home before has checked out for a minute. Many people love their bullshit more than they love their spouses, or at least they'll defend their bullshit more fiercely. If you've ever questioned a true believer about astrology or UFOs or the existence of weapons of mass destruction in Iraq, you know the danger of calling bullshit. Your believer will take your skepticism personally, and may even start regarding you as The Enemy.

Feminists call bullshit on the widespread but inaccurate belief that male dominance is the proper social order, and needless to say, this belief is more widespread than even the belief in astrology or WMDs in Iraq. So if you're a feminist, you're facing a lot of hurt feelings. People don't want to hear your truth puncture their fantasies.

With all the downsides, why not go along with the flow of bullshit and let someone else be the truth-speaker out there? Well, you probably wouldn't be holding this book if you weren't already a feminist, so odds are you already know your own story of how you moved from fear to feminism. And odds are you have already learned the dirty little secret of bullshit-callers from time immemorial, which is that calling bullshit, once you have a little practice, is pretty fun. Once you quit letting bullshit rule your life, you're much freer in a lot of ways. Plus, a lot of bullshit-callers do not suffer fools well, so even if we wanted to avoid calling bullshit, we're compelled to do it and have just learned to like it.

I consider myself a member of the compulsive category of bullshit-callers. Not that I shook my rattle angrily or anything, but just about. From disbelieving the lie that if you ignore bullies they'll just go away to telling my mother that Santa Claus wasn't real at an early age, I've had a lifelong problem of not being able to play along with rancid-smelling bullshit. People often ask me how it is that I managed to grow up deep in the underpopulated red-state patriarchy of West Texas and still grow into a loudmouthed feminist, and I wish I had a better story for them, but I don't have any such fascinating tale. I was just born with my eyes rolling. I've no doubt that one day they'll have some sort of medication regimen to cure cradle-to-grave cynics, but in the meantime, we skeptical feminists need to survive.

As a survival guide, this book has three main themes, touched on in various ways throughout: how to spot sexism, how to resist it, and how to have fun fighting back against it, the last being perhaps the most critical skill. Spotting sexism sounds easy, but the sheer commonness of it, coupled with its surprising diversity, makes it so that even hardened feminists could use refreshers. Many a feminist has said to herself, "Why does situation X bother and frustrate me so much?" only to realize at some later date that it seemed unfair and stupid because it was stupid, unfair sexism. Resisting sexism is the fine art of getting through the bullshit without breaking blood vessels in your face from the stress tension. Fighting back is a step up from resistance, of course, though both are legitimate survival strategies, depending on your situation.

The last question I want to address is "Who are you to write this book?" It's a tad coy but completely accurate to note that I'm a surviving feminist. I made the transition from mostly resisting to regularly fighting back almost by accident. In 2004, I created the blog Mouse Words as a place to resist. I wanted to blow off steam, record my thoughts about feminism (among other things), and maybe communicate with a few fellow travelers. It served its purpose almost too well, and next thing I knew, a blogger named Jesse Taylor was inviting me to join him at his much bigger blog Pandagon. The audience for my writing grew tremendously, and before I knew it, I and my fellow feminist blogging travelers weren't just resisting anymore, we were officially fighting back, making news, rallying the troops, and having an effect.

Suffice it to say, you make that kind of splash, and you have to survive quite a bit of bullshit, from random sexist trolls clogging up your blog comments to, as it turned out in my case, a national campaign against you to discredit your name because of your firmly held pro-woman, pro-gay views (which is a story for another book). I've survived it, so I'm somewhat of an authority on it. More importantly, I've had fun surviving it, and I think that every feminist should.

So here's the guide on how to do it.

PART 1.

THE EMERGING FEMINIST: HIGH SCHOOL AND COLLEGE

Everything I Need to Know I Learned from Idolizing Female Country Stars

It's a sick obsession and I know I should abandon it, but it's hard. Many of them are Republicans. Many of them are badly educated rednecks. And pretty much all of them are sanctimonious Christians. But I love me some sassy female country music stars. And they are a source, for many a red state–surviving feminist, of tips on hanging in and kicking ass.

DOLLY PARTON

Song of note: "I Will Always Love You." This song was written as a tender farewell not to a lover, actually, but to an old musical partner, Porter Wagoner. She had been his second on his hit TV show for many years and when she decided to go solo, the common feeling was that she was going to fall flat on her face without him. This song was on her first album, which was a big hit and left no doubt that on her own, she was going to be a huge star.

Lesson learned: Loving men doesn't mean living in their shadow. Also, association of any sort with a Kevin Costner film can leave a stain of mediocrity that can take more than a decade to clean away.

TAMMY WYNETTE

Song of note: "Stand By Your Man," of course.

Lesson learned: Pious invocations of traditional moral values will always come back to bite you on the ass. Wynette may have not intended for the song to come off as scolding women about the feminine virtue of putting up with men's shit, but it was taken that way. And since she racked up five weddings in her short life, the song became something of a joke. It's too bad, since Wynette is an excellent songwriter.

JEANNIE C. RILEY

Song of note: "Harper Valley PTA," a massive hit about a mother who is scolded, in a note sent home with her daughter by the PTA, for wearing miniskirts and having affairs. She then shows up at the PTA and exposes all the hidden scandals of the members.

Lesson learned: Pretty much all scolds are hypocrites, and the best thing you can do is tell them to shove it.

LORETTA LYNN

Song of note: "The Pill," a song that was roundly banned by various radio stations.

Lesson learned: There's more to life than being constantly pregnant, for one thing. For another, saying so out loud pisses people off.

KITTY WELLS

Song of note: "It Wasn't God Who Made Honky Tonk Angels," an answer song to Hank Thompson's "The Wild Side of Life." It ended up being much more popular than the song it was answering.

Lesson learned: As soon as you start standing up to men who want to blame women for everything that goes wrong, things will start looking up for you. Yes, even in record sales.

DIXIE CHICKS

Song of note: "Goodbye Earl." Before they became famous outside of country fandom for being crucified for speaking out against the Iraq war, they had already pissed off many conservative country fans with this song about two good friends who plot to kill one's abusive husband.

Lesson learned: Only through collective action can we overturn the oppressive patriarchy. Also, extracurricular high school activities like 4-H can be valuable career-enhancing experiences.

The Silver Ring Thing

Much apologies for my great state of Texas, and in this case on behalf of the city of Lubbock. Lubbock is a fine town for being the home of Buddy Holly, but unfortunately, its other major contribution to American culture is its insistence on the old-fashioned idea—known as the Lubbock Principle—that the only proper reaction to having things occur in your community that make you uncomfortable is to have the government ban those things. Whether or not this is effective, or correct, or even whether or not those laws make the situation worse are all irrelevant to the Lubbock Principle. The most famous example of the Lubbock Principle is the ban on selling alcohol inside the city limits. This law hasn't done a damn thing to stop or even slow down drinking in the city, but it has created a district right outside the city limits that provides alcohol to the residents. As an added bonus, it means that people who go out drinking spend that much more time on the road after imbibing. Clearly, the Lubbock Principle is good for self-righteous preening, but not so good for actually tackling social problems.

Unsurprisingly, we have the Lubbock Principle to thank for the political and social nightmare known as "abstinence-only education." In the '80s and '90s, most of West Texas was operating under the sex education principle of pretending there was no such thing as sex, but the city of Lubbock, never content to let a bad idea go without making it worse, was where it was decided to add jewelry to the whole equation. And so the Silver Ring Thing was born.

Friends of mine who lived in Lubbock at the time the Silver Ring Thing was emerging confirm the worst suspicions about it. The idea behind it is that one can easily persuade young women to play into the patriarchy by offering them baubles. The Oooh, Shiny theory of extracting female compliance with sexist norms wasn't something the patriarchy fans pulled out of their collectives asses, to be fair. The widespread cultural fascination with engagement rings alone is all the evidence you need to prove that bribery works.

For those who don't know what the Silver Ring Thing is, it's simple. Girls are given silver rings and in exchange they vow to stay virgins until they marry. Jesus Christ usually figures into this, but since the program now receives government funding, the religious elements have supposedly been scrubbed out. However, the creepy purchase of your hymen for a piece of cheap jewelry is still central to the whole thing. Worse, it's being packaged as education.

According to my friends who suffered through it, refusing to get tagged with a Virgin Ring is pretty hard for girls to do. Typically, the abstinence promoters will send the already marked virgins out to recruit. Being asked by a female friend to pledge your virginity is a fraught occasion, since saying yes means you have to stand in front of a roomful of people and discuss what you plan to do with your hymen in great detail. Saying no means your friend will be alarmed at your nascent slutitude and may even start rumors about you that could lead to local jocks asking if it's true that you'll suck a cock for a Coke.

The situation is such a losing one for the girl approached that there's only really two ways to respond.

1. Make your excuses. Say to your virginity petitioner, "Sorry, I would love to go promise my virginity to Jesus and get a silver ring, but it would just be dishonest. See, I've already bequeathed my maidenhead to Zod and marked the occasion with a clitoral piercing. It's cool! I even had it engraved with the words 'Kneel Before Zod.'" By the time you're halfway through offering to show off your piercing to your virginity-pushing friend, she'll be hightailing out of there and back to church.

2. Agree to do it. But write your own virginity vows so that you are literally vowing to hang on to your virginity until Jesus returns to take it. This is the best option if you are fairly certain that you'll be at a ceremony that features people pruriently listening to others' virginity vows. Bonus points if you can get your own faith-based grant to promise Jesus his shot at your virginity.

Regardless of how you choose to handle it, if caught in the unfortunate situation of having someone pressure you to pledge your hymen for the good of the Lord, it's important to remember that abstinence-only education is not only unrealistic and homophobic (waiting until marriage to have sex leaves you out of luck if you're gay and can't get married), it's downright dangerous. Research shows that kids who take virginity pledges aren't likely to keep them, and also that kids who don't get information about safe sex are very likely to take unsafe chances.

So perhaps the best bet when someone approaches you about virginity pledges is to offer a trade—you'll listen to her and her church preach the virtues of abstaining until marriage, if she and her fellows will be open to getting comprehensive sex education and having a discussion of the antigay problems with the abstinence-until-marriage model.

Of course, that will probably get roughly the same reaction as pointing out that you already promised your virginity to Zod.

Dating Advice for the Fifteen-Year-Old

In April 2005, Dan Savage posted a column full of advice from women about what they wished they'd known about dating when they were fifteen. Some was good, and of course some was wretched. My friend Jill Filipovic suggested that feminist bloggers come up with their own advice. Here's mine.

1. Don't worry if you aren't dating—the tipping point for most people is sometime after sixteen. Once you start, there's gonna be a flood. Flood or drought will then be the rule of dating from here til whenever.

2. The boys who everyone thinks are the great catches in high school often become the biggest dipshits later. If you think they are dipshits now, you are ahead of the curve.

3. Go ahead and masturbate. No one cares.

4. Take some time to pull out a hand mirror and look at your vulva, as if you were a '70s housewife at a consciousness-raising group. It's corny, but it's important. Consider that men look at their own genitals multiple times a day but many women go months, years, or possibly their whole lives without doing so. This has got to mess with your worldview.

5. Decide right now to use protection when you have sex, even if it's years off. The more certain you are now, the more confident you'll be when it comes time to insist on it.

6. Dress as weird as you want and don't let your parents tell you that you're prettier if you look like Suzy Creamcheese. You have your whole life to look normal. And dressing like someone you're not will never attract the people you want.

7. Develop your own taste in books, movies, and music. Learn the difference between learning new things from guys you date and letting them dictate your taste to you. One day, and it is inevitable, someone will praise or mock an ex-boyfriend for not training your taste properly. Be sure enough of yourself not to put up with that bullshit.

8. If a boy acts like a dog to you, it's not your fault, no matter what anyone says.

9. Your first love really is love, even if everyone says that you have to be X age to love. You might have to be that old to marry or have kids. You are probably too young to pick 'em. Your love will probably die quickly because you go through so many changes at your age. None of this matters, because love is love. Don't get hung up on whether or not it's "real." If you fall in love with women, don't let anyone tell you it's just a phase. You may end up being a lesbian or bisexual, or you may end up identifying as straight. But what you feel is important regardless of age or gender.

10. All this will be a vague memory before you know it.

Purity Balls, or How Your Parents Can Help You Get a Book Deal

Texas may have to take responsibility for the virginity ring thing, but responsibility for the next level of creepiness rests on the backs of the Southern and Midwestern right-wing nuts who have started to promote abstinence until marriage by throwing father–daughter dances called purity balls. The entire existence of purity balls gives off a distinct creepy vibe, starting with the use of the word "purity," which is a word usually used to denote the cleanliness of consumer products like Ivory soap, suggesting that therefore women who have sex before marriage can be thrown out as impure, defunct commodities, sort of like how you toss out a box of cereal if you find an "impurity" like a roach or a fingernail in it. Then there's the fact that the girls dress up in prom dresses and go on "dates" to these balls with their fathers, where they then promise to keep their hymens intact for their fathers. A typical pledge from one girl to her father goes, "I pledge to remain sexually pure . . . until the day I give myself as a wedding gift to my husband. . . . I know that God requires this of me . . . that he loves me. And that he will reward me for my faithfulness."

The father in return promises to "cover" his daughter—i.e., protect her from having her hymen pierced by any stray boys just because she likes those boys and wants to have sex with them. The word "cover" is standard in these modern fundamentalist ceremonies and rites, and none of these fundamentalists seem to be aware of how creepy it sounds for a father to promise to cover his daughter to make sure that her vagina remains unfilled by unapproved organs. (Unapproved by him, that is. Her approval is irrelevant to the situation.)

As could be expected, these purity balls drew some feminist attention and ire, and one common complaint was the cheap shot, "Interesting that there's only purity balls for girls." Few wingnuts can pass up the opportunity to make a shallow attempt at appearing like they don't have a double standard even though they clearly do, and so the integrity ball was created. Integrity balls are purity balls with the sexes reversed, where mothers take their sons and try to entice them to stay virgins until marriage, but because we're in right-wing fundamentalist nut territory, the sexism is deep and pure.

First, there's the difference in the names. Integrity is a character trait, but the word "purity" implies that the main focus of the event is make sure the vagina is squeaky clean for a potential husband. More to the point, the focus of the integrity balls is on the . . . purity of the vagina. At one integrity ball held in South Dakota, the pastor Luke Baker cautioned the male attendees against sex before marriage lest they damage the purity of someone else's future wife-purchase, by saying, "So you're dating someone else's future wife. If you knew somebody was with your future wife, touching her in ways you wouldn't like, pressuring her, how would that make you feel?"

If you're a young woman and you find yourself in a situation where you're being pressured to attend a purity ball, there is reason to be optimistic. After all, if your father seems up for it, you now have the grounds to sue for emancipation, and you'll probably get it, even if you're only twelve years old. Purity balls have a creepiness factor high enough to alarm even the most conservative employees at Child Protective Services, so you have that going for you. After you get out and get as far away from home as possible, probably landing in a hip coastal city, then you have a nice shot at a book deal and some talk show appearances in your near future. So buck up and get to suing!

What to Do When *Girls Gone Wild* Comes Knocking

You have to admire the *Girls Gone Wild* series on the basis of capitalist ingenuity. Porn had hit something of a wall when it came to cutting labor costs, because of the selfish nature of women who wanted to get paid for their work when it came to getting naked for the camera. And then Joe Francis, founder of *Girls Gone Wild*, came up with a way to get around the problem—bring the cameras into situations where alcohol lowers inhibitions and a crowd of drunk guys can be relied upon to pressure women to take off their clothes. Under his scheme, labor costs for the talent got slashed to the price of the T-shirt or baseball cap you get after you get naked for *Girls Gone Wild*. Porn has been credited with driving innovation in the videotape industry and on the Internet, and now it can be credited with innovation in union-busting techniques before porn actresses and models even managed to unionize in the first place.

Regardless of your opinions on porn or on girls going wild, the combination of the two is most definitely a Bad Thing. (The sea of rape allegations and lawsuits over lack-of-consent issues that follow *Girls Gone Wild* only adds more evidence to the pile.) And expect that *Girls Gone Wild* will come to your town. The franchise needs an endless stream of naked boobies to stay afloat, and this means they tend to show up eventually in every town with a reasonable-size college and a bar that will host them. And what bar wouldn't, seeing as how the words "Girls Gone Wild" in its weekly advertisements will lure every drink-happy asshole in a one-hundred-mile radius?

A group of women in Bloomington, Indiana, have found an innovative way to shut down *Girls Gone Wild:* by showing up with their own cameras at bars where events are scheduled and making it clear to the bar owners that they will report any underage drinking they see. Considering that underage drinking is a critical part of a good deal of *Girls Gone Wild* porn-for-no-pay labor-gathering, this method has worked remarkably well. It's just the tip of the iceberg of ways to culture-jam *Girls Gone Wild.*

SHOW UP BEFORE THE CAMERA CREWS AND START HOSTING *GUYS GONE WILD*

Hire a bunch of male strippers and bring them to the bar to start "going wild" by getting naked and putting on a show for the women. Consider the possibilities: *Girls Gone Wild* shows up at the bar, only to find that the drunk assholes they rely on to exert pressure on young women have all fled the place in horror at the sight of some taut young men dancing naked and waggling their dicks at a crowd of appreciative women. The visual side benefits alone of this gag would make it worth it.

SHOW UP WEARING DISTINCTLY OFF-PUTTING CLOTHES AND FOLLOW THE CAMERAMEN AROUND, DEMANDING THE RIGHT TO GO WILD

Wearing full clown gear, right down to the baggy clothes, red noses, and white face paint would work well, but so would T-shirts that say JOE FRANCIS MUNCHES ASS. The main thing is to follow the cameramen around, begging and pleading to be in the show. Inject yourself in between them and anyone they've targeted, saying, "But we're so much hotter, c'mon!" If they're smart, they'll try to indulge you, but if that happens you can simply start doing something very silly or boring, like honking your noses or reenacting scenes from *My Dinner with Andre*. If they try to leave you during this, restart the whining and following them around.

COMPETE WITH *GIRLS GONE WILD* THE WAL-MART WAY

Undercut prices, in other words. Set up a party next door to where *Girls Gone Wild* is being filmed and give beer away for free or for the price of a cheap cover charge. Since you're not making a profit, it should only cost you the price of the kegs, especially if you can barter with the people who own the space on the theory that hosting *Girls Gone Wild* gives their competitors an unfair advantage. To sweeten the deal, you could always run filmstrips of erotic cartoons or have your local burlesque group do a show, so people get all sexed up without actually having to exert coercive pressure on young women. Just make sure to ban cameras at the door.

UNIONIZE, UNIONIZE, UNIONIZE

At the center of the *Girls Gone Wild* controversy is the issue of exploiting labor—why should Joe Francis get millions while the naked girls who made him famous get paid in T-shirts? In fact, that makes a great message for a sign you can put up next to your soapbox when you start to rally for a union and a strike. If you call yourself the Slut Union, you could have even more fun coming up with signs like Just Because I'm a Slut Doesn't Mean I'm Cheap or No Tits for T-shirts. Print up some union cards and have some friends help by creating a strike line in front of the club, where they can pass out fliers explaining why it's not fair for the women who do the work of getting naked to go without their pay. Accuse anyone who wants to go in and show her tits for free of being a scab. Since a lot of the people who populate the bars that host *Girls Gone Wild* are members of the more vapid sector of the college crowd, this could be a good stunt to educate people about the general point of unions, as well.

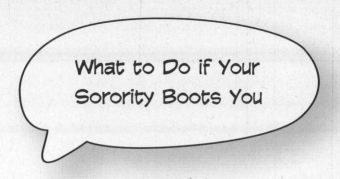

What to Do if Your Sorority Boots You

Hard as it may be to believe sometimes, the sisterhood can often be not very sisterly. That's what twenty-three of the members of the Delta Zeta sorority at DePauw University found out when they were ousted from the sorority in 2007. The ostensible reason for their ejection was that they weren't doing enough to recruit new members. Six more sisters, shocked that sororities lack in solidarity, quit in protest.

After a rudimentary examination of the shared qualities of those ejected and those who got to stay, it became clear that the closer you were to the racist, sexist ideal of the thin blonde, the more likely it was that you got to stay. The sorority had sisterhood the same way that Jerry Falwell has Jesus: as a cover story for the true patriarchal agenda. While this news—either about Falwell or about sororities—shouldn't be shocking, to some true believers, it can be a splash of cold water.

So if you suddenly find yourself getting thrown out of the sorority you thought for sure was going to be the one genuine sisterhood, remember these steps.

DON'T PANIC

What are you losing, after all? Not the sisterhood, as that's been shown to be a lie. At this point, you're losing your opportunity to wear ill-fitting sweatshirts with

Greek letters on them and possibly your opportunity to get routed to drunk frat boys as a humpable object.

PUT DOWN THE BOTTLE OF PEROXIDE

You may be thinking that a quick fix might be just the thing to keep you in the club. Don't be a fool. If the problem your sisters have with you could be fixed with a bottle of peroxide, they would have told you about it a long time ago. That bottle of Miss Clairol won't make your ass fit into a size 0, nor will it make you white. Peroxide certainly won't lower your IQ until you're less threatening to the yuppie assholes of tomorrow. Would you even want it to? Dye your hair if you want to, but know that it's not going to ingratiate you back into the backstabbing "sisterhood."

SPEAK TO THE MEDIA

This is where the ejected members of Delta Zeta shone. Everyone likes a catfight, so the media will want to talk to you. If exploiting the catfight mania of the mainstream media makes you uncomfortable, consider the greater good. You are, after all, exposing the more personal catfighting swipe that was taken at you for being nonwhite/wearing a size 8 or larger/using words with three syllables.

ATONE FOR YOUR PREVIOUS SORORITY SINS

Good on you if you didn't ever participate in bitching at other women for the crime of not cultivating the image of the perfect frat boy fuck toy. If you managed to get as far as you did in your shallow sorority without feeling like you needed to dog on other women, then you're a saint. Most of us would give in to the temptation to stay on our sisters' good sides by hating on women deemed unworthy.

If you're more typical, you have some atonement to do, now that you are on the receiving end of such abuse. You could find some typical ways to atone, such as volunteering at a soup kitchen or whatnot. Or you could give away all your expensive sorority girl clothes away at the Goodwill so someone broker can have them.

Whatever you do, don't hand off your boyfriend to someone you deem needy, even for one night. Amy Irving did that in *Carrie* and it didn't turn out so well for her.

SEEK OUT THE GENUINE SISTERHOOD

Surely there's a feminist group or two on your campus for you to join. Hand out condoms with the prosex feminists or protest rape with the antiviolence feminists. (Usually it's the same group anyway.) No one will hold it against you if you're not white or not super skinny or not stupid—in fact, diversity tends to be a strong point. Brains especially are a selling point, since activist communities could always use more bright people coming up with bright ideas.

Plus, the boys are less slobbery. Just as, if not more, importantly, the music is way better. Why listen to the same damn crappy '80s music that people didn't like the first time it came out when you can be shaking your newly feminist ass to Le Tigre? The dress code is better too. At least it's cheaper, once you abandon the need to wear makeup and high heels everywhere. Even sweatshirts get cheaper when you can buy them at Target instead of paying top dollar to get the ones with Greek letters on them.

Most importantly, your position in the feminist sisterhood is a tad more stable. When the goal is supporting women instead of supporting the cheap sexual tastes of trashy, spoiled frat boys, the amount of trust you have in your sisters miraculously goes up.

What Is It with *The Vagina Monologues?*

To hear your average wingnut speak it, the greatest threats to our nation, in order, are terrorism, the estate tax, and *The Vagina Monologues*. Yes, the play by Eve Ensler has wedged out "welfare queens" in the list of the greatest dangers to our way of life. When comparing the amount of ink spilled lamenting this play versus the amount of ink spilled on actual copies of this play, the former exceeds the latter by a factor of ten.

If you're a student, few things will bring out the wingnuts like staging a version of *The Vagina Monologues*. Antifeminist women's groups like the Independent Women's Forum and the Clare Boothe Luce Policy Institute loathe this play and the annual rounds of showing it at college campuses on Valentine's Day to protest violence against women. In fact, they loathe it so much that both groups have protests against the play every year, usually called "Take Back the Date."

The premise of "Take Back the Date" goes something like this: There was once a time where the grody frat boys of today were tuxedoed young men, eager to take young women on chaste but expensive dinner dates where they then would shower them with diamonds. Now such young men are irritating, drunken wretches who try to get their hands down your pants every chance they get.

The reason? Feminists. Feminists with copies of *The Vagina Monologues* in hand. Why this particular play was the end of financially appealing but sexually uninteresting dates is hard to say, but one suspects antifeminists believe that college men didn't know about vaginas, and therefore didn't know to start pawing at them as soon as the first beer was drunk, before the feminists, led by Eve Ensler, blew the whistle. Now young men are completely insufferable, and antifeminist women's groups want to get rid of the play, and hope that the next crop of young men never learn what a vagina is, thereby returning them to their innocent, tuxedos-and-roses status.

It might be a play worth staging regardless, since more people are familiar with the controversy than the play and might therefore be pleasantly surprised at how funny, entertaining, and yes, even thought-provoking it can be. But if you do it, remember that the Wingnut Factor is almost surely going to be an issue. There are good sides and bad sides to this.

DOWNSIDES
- The whining you will have to hear may take out an eardrum.
- There's a chance that some college Republicans who think they're clever will dress up like penises and dance around in random places on campus.
- The whining.

UPSIDES
- There's a chance that some college Republicans who think they're clever will dress up like penises and dance around in random places on campus, thereby proving to everyone how clever they're not.
- Seeing the word "vagina" on a marquee could be enough to send some wingnuts into fainting spells and even head explosions.
- Conservative students doing recon by viewing the play may learn what oral sex is, decide to try it once just to see what it is, realize what they've been missing, abandon their religion and their politics, and come to the light.

- You might be able to provoke the wingnuts into raising money for domestic violence shelters. This is not a joke; in order to "combat" the play at some schools, conservative student groups have held "Take Back the Date" events, and in order to make these hostile gestures a little more palatable, they've found they have to raise money for causes like fighting domestic violence to keep the media coverage from being completely negative.
- Students trying to find out what the hell "vagina" means may do some research, which could help fix some of the problems created by abstinence-only education.

Part 2.

FAMILY MATTERS

Conservative Relatives Discover Your Feminist Ways

If you come from more conservative stock and drift away into the realm of feminism, there will come a time when you'll be called to account for it to your family. You can put off the inevitable for a time, playing mum when people talk politics at dinner, smiling vacantly if someone asks if you liked the last episode of Bill O'Reilly's show, but you will get caught eventually. *Bitch* magazine will come in the mail while your mom is collecting it for you while you're on vacation. Or a pro-choice sticker will fall out of your handbag. Or someone will notice the woman-power tattoo on your forearm, and you'll be outed.

Now, you could make a big old stink about it and fight with your family tooth and nail over your feminist status, but who really wants to fight more with their families than absolutely necessary? Here are alternative strategies to preserve your sanity and your family.

SHAMELESS FLATTERY

Your average conservative thinks of himself as extremely independent-minded, so you can butter up your older relatives by highlighting how your quirky ways just demonstrate how well you learned the lesson of being independent and stubborn. Just try not to trip up and phrase it like, "Well, I learned all about sticking to my guns and doing my own thing like you taught me. Luckily, my independence didn't include lockstep compliance with right-wing talk radio."

RECRUIT THE WOMENFOLK

The patriarchy really screwed up by leaving women all alone to tend to the most thankless tasks, because women use that opportunity to talk to each other. I've discovered that cooking and doing dishes are the best places to hone your patriarchy-blaming skills, because that's where all the raw material really comes pouring out. Not only are you in a patriarchal situation, where women do housework while men laze around, but in this situation, you get to hear everything from feeling underappreciated by men to dealing with childcare and gynecological hassles. My experience also shows that you can work the word "sexism" into these conversations and find surprisingly positive results, so long as there aren't any men around. It's not consciousness-raising, but it's a start.

KICK THEIR ASSES AT SOME GAMES

If you're good at board games or video games, it can really quell the sexist carping to challenge your male relatives and kick their asses. Beware of this one, though, because you run the strong chance that someone will pull out the exception card and claim that you may be good, but you're an exception among women, and you'll get sucked back into battle.

USE YOUR FEMINIST STATUS TO SCARE YOUR RELATIVES OFF CERTAIN UNCOMFORTABLE LINES OF QUESTIONING

Don't want to talk about when you're getting married? Suggest to your relatives that you're too busy organizing a lesbian commune to get around to marriage. Bonus points if you are in fact organizing a lesbian commune. Don't want to answer questions about when you're having children? Tell them you have to reach your abortion quota before you even consider giving birth to a live one. If they're properly propagandized by conservative media to think of feminists as man-hating baby killers, these suggestions will sound mild compared to their worst fears.

ACT MYSTERIOUS

A lot of conservatives have grown accustomed to thinking that feminists belong to a secret society of women who conspire to create a matriarchy through strategic abortion. How this is supposed to work is hard to figure, but Rush Limbaugh said it and a lot of folks believe it. With this in mind, you have an opportunity to live out the fantasy of what it must be like to belong to a secret conspiracy. When around your conservative relatives, you don't have to be Jane Doe, average workaday voting liberal feminist. You're someone with a secret identity, just playing the part of the ordinary person with a family. Think 007 or a superhero or a mobster who goes home and doesn't talk about all the people he has to knock off in the course of a day's work. Give relatives who ask about your political activism a small, mysterious smile and shake your head slightly. If you're not going to convince them you're not in such a conspiracy, why not enjoy their belief that you are?

The Endless Discussion on the Nature of Housework, or How I Stopped Worrying and Learned to Love My Mop

The topic universally considered the most acid in feminism is porn. Porn drives so many people to distraction, from the pro- to the anti- to the maybe-porn views, that it actually became the famous focus of a series of "porn wars" in the '80s that threatened to rend feminism apart. And yet, I offer that there is a more treacherous topic to bring up in a feminist discussion forum, either in person or on the Internet, and that topic is housework.

At first, housework seems like it would not be a controversial issue. The statistics are clear. Women—even women who work as many hours on average as men—do twice as much housework as men, on average. Married women do more housework than single women, but single men do more housework than married men. That marriage tends to mean that women pick up more unpaid labor and men have to do less shouldn't create trauma, but just addressing this question as a problem and opening it up for discussion is enough to raise emotions to a boil and leave everyone involved mildly traumatized.

It's quite similar to the way that you can't bring up the topic of porn and sexism without sending a discussion into a tailspin. But if you think about it in any depth, it makes sense that these two would be equally contentious issues, since the only thing more personal than producing body fluids in front of the computer is cleaning body fluids off the toilet. Because of this similarity, the rhetorical ploys that get bandied around in both discussions, particularly the rhetorical ploys to minimize and ignore uncomfortable issues, are strikingly similar.

At the end of a good discussion about either porn or housework, there should be at least one man reconsidering his male privilege, but at least three or four women wondering why they haven't yet run off and joined a lesbian commune. (Mostly, they don't advertise in the Yellow Pages.) The topic frustrates, because no matter how many times it's chewed over in the mainstream media, on the blogs, and around dinner tables across the nation, at the end of the day women still do twice the housework men do and therefore have less time to pick their noses and read *War and Peace*.

RHETORICAL PLOY	PORN	HOUSEWORK
Not my Nigel!	My husband/boyfriend wouldn't watch porn/nasty porn!	My boyfriend actually takes out the trash when he's asked!
Gloating self-superiority	You are all sexually naive if you find this topic interesting at all.	My spouse and I live in perfect chore-sharing equality and we managed to get here without any tense discussions at all.
Blaming women	Porn makes women uneasy because women are such prudes.	Women are the ones who make up the standards, anyway, so they only have themselves to blame for working twice as hard.
Men cannot be expected to do better.	Asking men to think about the content and production of porn is the equivalent of forbidding them to get erect ever again.	Men don't see dirt.
Clueless dudes offer their opinions.	What's so wrong with naked ladies?	I mow the lawn once a week. Are you trying to suggest that the endless housework my wife does is harder than that?
How can we spin this to spare men from having to make changes?	Have you ever considered that having someone shoot come in your face and call you a "dirty whore" might be a compliment?	Perhaps if we all agreed to live in filth, this problem would go away.
The problem is solved by avoiding the issue.	Hide your porn.	Hire a maid.

What can be done to resolve this sticky issue? After spending a great deal of time pondering all the various solutions offered, I've narrowed it down to ones that could work.

MEN COULD CLEAN MORE

Start with the basics. Women clean more than men because men aren't doing their fair share. Men could clean more, leaving less for women to do.

MEN COULD RESOLVE TO CLEAN MORE, AND THEN END UP CLEANING MORE

One more step, thus slightly more complicated, but still within the realm of the possible.

WOMEN COULD CHALLENGE MEN TO CLEAN MORE, MEN COULD RESOLVE TO CLEAN MORE, AND THEN MEN COULD END UP CLEANING MORE

While this seems unnecessarily complicated, especially compared to the first solution, I've been assured that sometimes it has to go this way for anything to get better.

WOMEN COULD CLEAN LESS

People who have gone with this solution stand firm by it, such as my friend Lindsay, who says, "Slob is the new slut." Some more cynical feminists such as myself still wonder if the overall level of housework going down means that things equal out, or if men reduce their housework happily as women reduce theirs. Still worth a try, unless you have relatives who claim to be afraid to sit on your toilet and hold you and you alone accountable for their fears.

The Opt-Out Revolution

ow to get published in the *New York Times*, a multistep process:

1. Channel yuppie male fantasies about having a beatific housewife who gave up her career ambitions to dedicate all her intelligence and spark to the worthy goal of feeding you, keeping your house, bearing your towheaded darling children, and maintaining a figure worthy of the acronym MILF so all your friends can burn with jealousy.

2. Write this fantasy down on paper, assuring the readership that women want to comply with this fantasy more than anything else in the world.

3. Cash your check.

Lisa Belkin raised feminist ire in 2003 when she wrote an article called "The Opt-Out Revolution" that did just this. For me, it was hard to be angry without spiking it with a heavy dose of enthusiasm for her big brass balls. I myself would choke on the fear that someone would see through my transparent attempt at shamelessly flattering the next generation of would-be patriarchs, but Belkin knew the cardinal rule of getting published in the *New York Times,* which is never underestimate the elitists capacity to swallow ginormous piles of bullshit. Quite possibly she drew inspiration from the breathless *Times* coverage of Bush's lies about Saddam's nuclear arsenal; compared to that, a little *Leave It to Beaver* fantasizing was minor-league bullshit.

Was it true that there was a trend of professional women eagerly beating feet back home to push expensive strollers all day? Not really. Belkin's article was thoroughly debunked in the left-leaning media, most notably by Joan C. Williams, who wrote a research paper for the University of California Hastings Center for WorkLife Law that detailed how women are mostly shoved out of work more than opting out. Still, the damage was done and the ideal of the Hot Soccer Mom more deeply embedded in the national consciousness. To drive home the point, the *Times* ran another article in 2005 by Louise Story that claimed women were so eager to apply their college degrees to the apron and the bassinet that Yale women were planning for it as undergrads. Story's article was also debunked, even by some of the Yale women she quoted, but again, the fantasy was reinforced.

We as a nation get what we deserve. After eight years of having a president with a hardworking lawyer for a wife, we elected a bumbling Yale graduate whose wife quit her job the second she married him, and this was supposed to be a good thing. If you already buy into the idea that there's any benefit to awarding George W. Bush his own wife-servant to cater to him, then it's not much of a stretch to extend that expectation to the nameless everyday female strivers currently populating college campuses.

At this point in time, mere rejection of Hot Soccer Momdom is not enough. The role has become so entrenched it needs people to approach it with a subversive eye toward camp. Getting into campy lampooning of the whole Soccer Mom fantasy could become the next big thing, a genuine opt-out revolution in garish colors. Soccer Moms have more materialism attached to them than any other silly feminine stereotype in history, so not camping it up is criminal.

Places to start:

BUY YOURSELF A SUBURBAN ASSAULT VEHICLE AND KEEP A COLLECTION OF GRISLY SOUVENIRS ON THE FRONT BUMPER

What are those things for anyway, if not to mow down little kids who might be competing with your precious little Your Husband Jr. for a starting position on the Little League team? Stuff and mount fake corpses of people who piss you off and had to be run over on your front bumper, from your children's scholastic rivals to your first college boyfriend who liked to smoke cigarettes and suggested that you elope after all those years of collecting bridal magazines. Adhere a bumper sticker that says You'll Pry My Chevy Tahoe from My Cold, Dead Hands. Make sure to slap a giant yellow ribbon next to it, to demonstrate your support for those sweet kids overseas protecting your ability to keep fuel in your tank.

Extra bonus points if you can get your hands on an actual tank.

THROW A CAPRI PANTS BEAUTY CONTEST CALLED "MILFIEST ANKLES"

The struggle between the pressure to be at all times maternal, sexy, and the epitome of WASPy slenderness has resulted in the unseemly popularity of high-water pants cutely called capri pants. Some come in khaki, but most come in garish flower prints that have matching tops. The capri pant allows you to show off a well-turned ankle without wearing anything sexy enough to get the PTA tongues wagging. It's the essence of MILF wear, and it's asking to be lampooned in a beauty pageant.

Contestants could enter the stage by emerging from a Lexus SUV parked onstage, sticking out their hot-'n'-sexy ankles first to wow the audience before emerging to show off the entire cotton-blend outfit that is both figure-flattering and not overly sexual. During the talent portion, contestants could demonstrate their skills, in turn, of corralling three kids under age six in the grocery store, cutting people off in traffic, and driving two hundred yards to the school in traffic to pick up their children.

LATTE-OFFS

In the long-ago Mayberry rural American past, the grain grew high, children behaved themselves, people went to church, and life was painfully boring. To rectify some of this boredom, people started to escalate the mundane details of life into competitive sports and traffic-stopping skills. Thus the existence of bakeoffs, hog-calling, cow patty bingo, and chasing greased pigs.

The slow, boring avenues of suburbia could use some of this spirit. You already know how to order a skinny extra-wet chai crème cappuccino grande without breaking a sweat or pausing for breath, so why not make it a competitive sport? Latte-ordering could be the Soccer Mom version of auction-calling, if you play your cards right.

IT'S SUPPOSED TO BE A REVOLUTION, SO START THE ARMY

The provocative name "Opt-Out Revolution" doesn't quite bring to mind a set of Soccer Moms jostling for the shortest line at the supermarket. Revolutions need armies, so why not start one? What could look both cooler and more cheesy than a line of identical black SUVs with gun turrets on the top and the words SOCCER FOREVER in menacing red paint gracing the sides? It would feel good to have people be afraid that any minute now, you're going to whip the sun cover off that stroller and pull out your AK-47. Granted, it's hard to determine who to fight when you're revolting on the basis of opting out, but that's no reason not to cover yourself in the allure of the warrior.

> ## Being the Vegetarian at the BBQ

Not all feminists are vegetarians, and rumor has it, though this hasn't been confirmed, that not all vegetarians are feminists. Still, it's well understood that vegetarianism and feminism are linked, to the degree that ordering the veggie burger instead of the regular burger at a restaurant can prompt people to ask you if you're working for NARAL now or what. As such, any vegetarian will tell you that the mere act of not eating meat at some gatherings will set some of your dining companions off on a tailspin of anxieties. You may not intend with your veggie burger or salad to politicize dinner in such an intimate way and make your friends or relatives have psychosexual episodes involving everything from their weight and health anxieties to the gender issues tied to what you eat. (Summary: Beef Is Man Food, Lettuce Is Woman Food. That women live longer on average than men has nothing to do with this, according to the national beef lobby.) To make up for the anxieties you provoke by abstaining from meat-eating, you will be subjected to a great deal of nosy questions.

HOW DO YOU GET ENOUGH PROTEIN?

Apparently, most people are under the impression that all human beings are growing all the time at an absurdly high rate and if you don't consume four pounds of protein a day, you'll be falling behind. I remind people that I've been the same height since the eighth grade, so if I had any more growing to do, I think it probably would have happened already.

HOW DO YOU AVOID BEING ANEMIC?

Just kidding. No one ever asks this, possibly because it's actually an issue for vegetarians, so this question fails the Utter Ignorance test that questions have to pass in order to be wielded at vegetarians snacking on cheese sandwiches at BBQs.

DO YOU EAT CHICKEN?

It's true that chickens are very dumb, but that doesn't make them vegetables. If we started demoting animals to vegetable status based on intelligence, then vegetarians would have the right to cannibalize everyone who thought *Everybody Loves Raymond* was an instant classic. Sitcom fans should rest easy, though, because vegetarians, as the name would imply, don't eat chicken.

ARE YOU DOING THIS FOR POLITICAL OR HEALTH REASONS?

This might be the worst question, because in a social situation, there's nothing much you can say that won't break some etiquette rule. Mumble and run, maybe. Excuse yourself to go to the bathroom. Say, "Both, and it's so very complicated and would take so long to explain that I don't want to bore you good people with it." Actually answering the question is out of the question unless you're oblivious to the fact that anything you say will be perceived as a judgment on people who don't share your political convictions or have arteries as squeaky-clean as yours.

Or you could avoid the question altogether and say, "Neither. I don't eat meat because it speaks to me and that wigs me out." Use only with people who don't have the power or inclination to have you committed.

DO YOU WANT JUST A LITTLE OF THIS [MEAT-BASED DISH]?

Americans are obsessed with contextualizing everything in terms of temptation and sin. Thus, vegetarians are assumed to be living this life where unbearable temptation beckons at every corner. Whether you do feel any temptation to eat meat or not, understand that the person waving the meat under your nose and begging you to eat thinks of herself as a temptress. She wants you to sin. She will enjoy watching it. She's never going to have the chance to get schoolkids hooked on crack, so this is her walk on the wild side. The question is, do you give her the pleasure?

Well, that's your call, but remember, this is a person who is fantasizing about giving crack to schoolkids, even if she doesn't realize it. Do you really want to indulge such a fantasy?

> # The Wedding-Industrial Complex: Don't Get Recruited, Since No One Makes Officer

ccording to industry estimates, the average wedding in America now costs $27,000. That's the down payment on a house, and all for a dress you'll never wear again, food you mostly won't eat, a DJ who plays a bunch of corny music, and the opportunity to have your friends, relatives, and neighbors pass judgment on your taste and find it wanting. In addition, you get to live under nonstop pressure to make everything perfect (or people will say you must not really be that much in love), but if you actually take the bull by the horns and start making the demands to make everything perfect, your reward is being called a "bridezilla" by people snickering at you over your silly, feminine intemperate ways.

So why do women do it? Rebecca Mead, in the May 9, 2007, edition of the *New York Times*, offered a theory.

> *"Getting married is still a big thing, but the transition is not the traumatic thing that it used to be," she said. "I think there is a way in which the trauma of the wedding planning is substituting for the trauma of the newlywed. People feel they have to go through some type*

of traumatic experience to show that they're married, to show that there is something different about them."

It's alluring to think that the trauma of losing your mind over the wedding replaces the traditional single-to-married tradition of traumatizing the bride through dramatic hymen removal, and there might be something to the theory. Mead's cagey use of the word "people" aside, everyone knows that the trauma of throwing a wedding belongs mainly to the bride, unless we're prepared to pretend there's something traumatic for a man in showing up to a big party thrown just for him where his main duty is showing up and allowing someone to pin a flower to his lapel. Sure, a handful of grooms-to-be will take on some planning responsibilities, but wandering any bridal expo will disabuse you of any notion that the percentage of grooms into responsibility-sharing goes beyond the single digits.

I prefer the theory that the growing wedding–industrial complex is a matter of capitalism meeting the sort of backlash against feminism Susan Faludi describes in *Backlash*. It has this entire payback element to it—sure, you women are allowed your jobs and your education and your birth control pills, but in exchange you have to be dressed up and tossed down the aisle like a virgin being thrown into the volcano. And help fuel the economy of the wedding–industrial complex while you're at it, as well.

Still, avoiding the entire shebang can be difficult, if you have friends and relatives pressuring you to throw a big party so they can gloat about your wedding and drink your booze. If you're so inclined to put them off, here are some ways to do so.

CLAIM THAT IF YOU MUST HAVE A FORMAL WEDDING, YOU WANT IT TO BE REALLY FORMAL

When people pressure you to get to marrying and providing them the pleasure of an expensive, formal wedding, get really excited about the idea. Suggest that everyone wear floor-length gowns and that the music be nothing but chamber music played by a live quartet. Deprived of the opportunity to dance the Chicken Dance and act like asses to "YMCA," many people lose their enthusiasm.

CLAIM THAT IF YOU MUST HAVE AN EXPENSIVE WEDDING, IT'S GOING TO BE REALLY EXPENSIVE

Fantasize out loud about holding your wedding in a five-star hotel in Tokyo. Reassure your friends that if you do it that way, they won't have to get you any other gifts besides being at your wedding—and paying for their own flights and hotel stays in Tokyo. Watch the pressure to have an expensive wedding dry up.

TELL THEM YOU COULDN'T GET MATCHING DRESSES

Lesbians are no longer exempt from the wedding–industrial complex. Gay cash spends as good as straight cash, and the industry isn't going to refrain from pressuring lesbians to have big, fancy weddings just because the state won't honor the actual marriages. If you're feeling the heat to make your relationship semiofficial, you could tell people you don't want to get married until it's legal, but that just means that if they do legalize marriage, the pressure to dump $27,000 of your very own will escalate.

So just coyly claim that no dressmaker will sell matching dresses, and if you can't do it right, you won't do it at all. While there are many comebacks to this, particularly if you're not overly fond of wearing dresses anyway, the comment will throw questions off long enough for you to make your escape.

Actually, if you're straight, the matching dresses excuse works even better to confuse people.

INSIST ON HAVING A NONTRADITIONAL WEDDING

Make sure to clarify how nontraditional you want to be—nothing clichéd like getting married by Elvis for *you*. No marching down the aisle to calliope music.

Instead of the father giving away the bride, she gives away her large ficus tree to him. When the minister says, "You may kiss the bride," the groom kisses her feet. Make the garter toss more literal and have the groom throw the bride's diaphragm. For the dinner service? Fondue. If your friends still pester you for a wedding after that, it might be worth it just to follow through.

If your efforts to run off the wedding pressure don't work—or you get the hankering to have that wedding with a $27,000 price tag for reasons of your own—don't forget to remember that the right to marry isn't extended to everyone. If you're lucky enough to have a legally allowed mixed-gender marriage, you might want to request, in lieu of gifts, donations to organizations dedicated to the rights of gays and lesbians.

Murphy Brown May Have Been Canceled, but Her Demonic Presence Lingers

Dan Quayle fired off the warning shot in a 1992 speech by invoking the nightmare of undersexed white men everywhere—the pretty white professional woman who opts out of getting married and instead has a baby on her own, depriving some white professional man of his white professional entitlement to regular sex and housework. Quayle claimed he only brought it up because of single mothers on welfare, who apparently have an obligation to be unhappily married that the Murphy Browns of the world don't have, but in truth, he was more interested in sending the signal that all women, regardless of salary or race, are born with the obligation to be married, no matter how unhappily, if they want to be mothers. And the right-wing nuts of the world listened, and since have spent the past fifteen years routinely claiming that all social ills derive from women who don't think they need to be tied to men who make them miserable, with a baby functioning as the leash.

The old blues-song phrase to convey woefulness was to claim to feel like a "motherless child," but in the world of the wingnuts, the only tragedy is to be a "fatherless child"—a phrase that assumes that the only way to really be a father is to live with the mother and lord over her with your male authority. Not that every marriage is "traditional," but mostly that's due to the fact that the single mother–bashing brigade hasn't figured out yet how to separate egalitarian marriages from nonegalitarian ones to bash egalitarian ones properly.

If you're a single mother or are thinking of becoming one through divorcing or simply not going through the preliminaries of marriage before having a kid, you're probably already aware of all the complaints against you. But here's a rough summary of all the myths about single motherhood employed to demonize you.

SINGLE MOTHERS ARE THE CAUSE OF POVERTY

Single mothers tend to live in poverty more than anyone else, and by the magic of conflating causation with correlation, social conservatives claim that all said single mothers need to do is get married and voilà! They'll morph into June Cleaver. This theory drives the marriage initiative created by the Bush administration in order to spend federal welfare money on anything but feeding and housing the poor. The bill diverted money from welfare into teaching single mothers how important marriage is. This package of cash-driven condescension didn't include eligible and willing husbands-to-be. You're supposed to find one of those on your own, and it's supposed at the outset you didn't think about that already. No money is included for babysitters so you can go out on dates to get this husband you need. But after a few courses in valuing the nonexistent good-provider husband, some wingnut magic and a little bit of pixie dust will bring him into your household, briefcase and gray suit included.

Luckily, thanks to the conservative rule "An unexamined premise is not worth disturbing," it's never asked if it might be harder for people living in poverty to hold their relationships together when there are potential fights about money around every corner.

SINGLE MOTHERS ARE THE CAUSE OF CRIME

Through more conflating causation and correlation, conservatives treat single motherhood as a cause of crime, independent of the linkage between poverty and crime. Of course, single motherhood is also singled out as the cause of poverty, so maybe it's the one case where conservatives will tacitly admit a linkage, though they'd prefer to think boys with single mothers are growing up to be criminals because Daddy didn't spank them enough. Example from W. Bradford Wilcox, writing for the *National Review* over Mother's Day weekend in 2007: "Mothers who manage to get and stay married are much less likely to produce boys who end up terrorizing playgrounds, parks, and little old ladies walking home from the grocery store."

Unfortunately, we never did learn if Murphy Brown's infamous baby grew up to knock over a liquor store. We'll just have to assume with good faith that he did.

SINGLE MOTHERS ARE THE CAUSE OF MENTAL ILLNESS

From the same Wilcox article: "Children who are fortunate to grow up with a married mother and father are much less likely to find themselves in serious emotional trouble. By contrast, children who grow up without their father are significantly more likely to suffer from depression." Apparently, grown men radiate happiness vibes into their children, but these magic powers can only be activated by the presence of a wedding ring. (Who knew your local mall jeweler sold rings with activation powers of the sort you thought only existed in fantasy fiction?) As an argument to convince women who are supposedly boycotting marriage to get married, this one is particularly silly. Unless, of course, you assume that huge percentages of women are forgoing their own and their children's happiness by stubbornly refusing good marriages.

I kind of liked it better when they were blaming mental illness on Satanic messages you could hear if you played heavy metal records backward. Bad as it was to give young people rebelling against hysterical Christian parents a reason to listen to crappy heavy metal, at least the damage stayed restricted to stickers stuck on the front of CD cases. Also, there was more comedy value in someone earnestly playing an LP backward than in someone earnestly poring over social statistics in an effort to find some science behind his sexism.

CHILDREN WHOSE PARENTS AREN'T MARRIED
ARE "FATHERLESS"

One of the more man-hating myths of the traditionalist crowd. The term "fatherless" crops up routinely in single mother–bashing literature, a word that implies that a father who isn't married to a mother must have disappeared into the oblivion or passed away (possibly overwhelmed by the army of germs that ate him up without June Cleaver present to wash his underwear). This term is so prevalent that it became the title of a prominent pro-patriarchy scaremongering book by David Blankenhorn, called *Fatherless America*. People drop it without pausing to think about how it may just be an insult to fathers who don't evaporate into the atmosphere without a wedding ring to secure them to our plane of existence.

One day, after reading column after column and website after website about The Fatherless, aka the children of unmarried mothers, I decided to call my own father, who is not married to my mother.

"Dad," I said when he answered the phone, "did you know that I'm 'fatherless'?"

This gave him pause. On one hand, he is a fan of Fox News and talk radio, and probably has familiarized himself quite well with the argument that single motherhood and "fatherlessness" is the cause of all social evils. On the other hand, he could in fact verify that he was sitting there on the phone talking to me. He also had ready access to a number of photographs demonstrating the physical resemblance between us, further evidence that he may indeed be my father, making me fatherful instead of fatherless.

Reason won him over. "Well, who would say such a thing? I'm right here, aren't I?" Indeed he was.

Having cleared up the inanity of the term "fatherless" to describe people like myself, I tried to clarify my language by calling myself a "bastard," but people had no idea whatsoever what I meant by that. Some old habits pass gently into the good night.

MOTHERS ARE TO BLAME WHEN MEN DON'T
FATHER THEIR CHILDREN

This myth has much cachet with various "fathers' rights" organizations, which exist mainly for men to present organized resistance against the horrors of child support. Since refusing to pay your child support is a time-honored way to make your children turn on you, it's no wonder that these organizations cast around looking for any half-baked alternate explanation. These groups peddle the theory that children who have issues with their fathers are suffering from "parental alienation syndrome"—a syndrome caused by women who brainwash their children into hating their innocent fathers, particularly those who have done the heroic deed of refusing to pay child support—which is as recognized by the American Psychological Association as "pulledfromuranus syndrome" is.

SINGLE MOTHERS ARE THE SOURCE OF ALL THAT
SHITTY MUSIC KIDS LISTEN TO THESE DAYS

Mary Eberstadt, writing for the Hoover Institution's December 2004 *Policy Review,* deserves a wingnut award for her creativity in the art of bashing single mothers. In her article "Eminem Is Right," she argues that not only can single mothers be blamed for poverty and crime, they can also be held responsible for much of the crappy music of the past decade. Granted, she pointed to maudlin songs about divorce by Papa Roach, Everclear, Blink-182, and Good Charlotte as evidence that a generation of young people disapproves of divorce (though there's no evidence indicating whether all of these young men—and they are all men—actually oppose divorce or are just mining it for lyrical ideas), and she doesn't say much about the quality of the music. But then again, she didn't have to, because most readers could draw an inference. Raise a kid without a husband in the house, and you're running the risk he'll grow up to be in a band like Good Charlotte. Best not take the risk.

THE PENIS IS THE THING

Liberals will happily admit that having two incomes and having two adults to split the work around the house probably does make child-rearing easier and more affordable, so often in discussions about single motherhood, we'll concede that point happily. No one disputes that ideal situations are better than nonideal situations, and having help around the house is better than not. But the benefit of two incomes and two pairs of hands is not what conservatives have in mind when they attack single mothers. Whether or not you can be a good mother is wound up in whether or not you regularly encounter a cock associated with someone you're in a legal entanglement with.

For instance, Janice Crouse of Concerned Women for America defined Mary Cheney, the lesbian daughter of Vice President Dick Cheney, as a "single mother," even though Mary's life partner might beg to differ with that designation.

> *Mary Cheney is among that burgeoning group of adult women over age twenty that are driving the trend of women who don't want a man in the picture, but want to have a baby. . . . As they grow older, fatherless children tend to have trouble dealing with male authority figures. Too often children in single-mother households end up angry at their absent fathers and resentful of the mother who has had to be a father figure, too.*

No penis, no pass. Crouse never did say how she felt about gay men who adopt children, and whether or not double the cock meant double the parenting magic. I doubt, however, she'd feel that way. You need one man to exude that traditional family magic that turns our tumultuous world into a shadow of a sitcom from the '50s, and one woman to do the cleaning, cooking, cocksucking, and child-rearing, or else you run the risk that the magic man will run off.

Of course, if your husband does leave you in the middle of the night, rest assured that it's all your fault.

Child Pressure, or Why You Don't Have to Kick Your Womb into Production (Right Away) Just Because You Have One

Why do people feel the need to pressure young women to have children? If you're young and cute or smart or really just female, and your stomach remains stubbornly flat past some appointed age, expect the pressure to kick in—from friends, from relatives, from strangers, and, of course, from the mainstream media. People just feel entitled to have babies to coo at without having to do the diaper-changing work themselves, and if you're perceived as a woman not doing her part in providing cute babies for others to coo at, you can expect complaints.

I also blame the deep human need to mess things up. Just as it's hard to walk by a row of dominoes without pushing it over, it's hard to walk by a flat female stomach without pressuring the owner to get to inflating it, and not with beer. Even staunchly pro-choice people succumb to the urge to needle childless young women to make babies, even though they know, intellectually, that most women currently not procreating have a good reason to avoid it. Maybe you're waiting for the right guy or for the chance to move out of your studio apartment or to reach the five-year mark with your McEmployer, when your health insurance kicks in. Maybe you never want kids, due to your allergy to sippy cups.

Yes, people know you probably have a good reason. But in far too many people the stimulus of seeing a never-pregnant woman creates an override switch between their brains and their mouths, and even though they know better, the words will come spilling out: "So are you planning on having a baby anytime soon?"

What to say?

"I can't."

Yes, it seems a little cruel to hit people with the humiliating stinger right off the bat, especially if you feel it's something of a lie to say that you can't, which implies that you may not have the physical capability to procreate, which you very well may have. But it doesn't have to be a lie if you view it in the right frame of mind! Hear me out.

You really can't have a baby anytime soon. After all, you're not pregnant, are you? So having a baby is, at bare minimum, nine and a half months away, and that's if you just so happen to run right home to find an erection-sporting man who doesn't mind skipping the condom *and* you're currently ovulating. So, you quite literally can't have a baby anytime soon, depending on your definition of "soon." Not a lie at all.

Plus, people who pressure random young women to have babies deserve to feel really bad about it on occasion, just as people who grab strange women's stomachs and ask when they're due deserve to have at least one woman rear up all offended and say, "Good sir, you've mistaken me for someone pregnant!" It might make them reconsider their bad habits next time.

Unfortunately for young women who don't feel particularly warm toward baby pressure, the duty of exerting it has fallen off the shoulders of nosy uncles and onto the sturdy shoulders of the mainstream media. A 2002 study showing that women's fertility begins to decline slowly starting at age twenty-seven became a minor media dustup, with the nuances of the study falling away in favor of alarmist articles that implied, strongly, that you can start expecting hot flashes at twenty-five and kiss away your last grasp on female fertility before you hobble across the thirty-year-old line. Being thirty myself, I was much disappointed to find out that the articles implying that I went through menopause three years ago were a tad off in their calculations. So much the better for Tampax's bottom line.

The early twenty-first century's queen bee in the art of chastising women for not getting pregnant early and often is most definitely Sylvia Ann Hewlett. In 2002, Hewlett published a book titled *Pretending That Anecdote Is Data*. No, wait—it was actually titled *Creating a Life: Professional Women and the Quest for Children*. Hewlett had keyed into one of the great ironies of our time, realizing that for white career women like herself, few roads to success are more certain than picking a career of bashing white women for behaving, well, like men, and making their careers a priority.

Hewlett cobbled together some anecdotal evidence that some women regret not getting married and having children in the past, and let the implication that women are too big for their britches do all the work of ushering her down a red carpet onto every talk show under the sun. If you enjoy dark, embittered humor, you could do worse for a source of it than watching daytime talk shows unsubtly chastise women for daring to have careers. Watching a couple of polished white career women on TV wring their hands over the tragedy of career women who don't understand that they'd be much happier with the June Cleaver lifestyle will make any feminist briefly long for the days when women were just expected to fetch the coffee to justify their existence in the workplace, because that at least was more dignified. Watching Katie Couric and Sylvia Ann Hewlett discuss the dangers that are lurking, fertility-wise, for career women reminded me vividly of Katherine's speech about the importance of blind obedience to husbands at the end of *The Taming of the Shrew*.

When faced with the media onslaught of guilt for establishing a career before committing to Marriage 'n' Babies, look to the general female population for a model on surviving. Despite the royal treatment Hewlett received in promoting her book in the mainstream media, copies stayed stubbornly on the shelf, selling less than ten thousand copies two months after the enormous blitz, according to Warren St. John in the *New York Times*. It turned out that the male-dominated media guessed a tad incorrectly when it gambled that women would want nothing more than to plunk down $22 a pop to be told that wanting a career made them failures as women.

Part 3.
SURVIVING THE SEXUAL MINEFIELD

The Hairy, Scary World of Mainstream Dating Advice

Wading into the land of mainstream dating advice is a dangerous endeavor, and I wouldn't recommend it to the fainthearted. But if you do, be prepared to visit a world with strong, noticeable differences from the real world you live in, a world where:

1. All people are heterosexual.

2. Men and women are creatures so utterly different from each other in every way that it's disputable that both could be considered carbon-based life forms.

3. People routinely desire the opportunity to live out their lives with partners wholly unlike themselves in every major way and are bewildered as to why this seems to cause problems.

The blame for this sorry situation lies with our capitalistic publishing system. Which is to say that people really enjoy reading about this fantasy world, and the closer the writer hews her advice to these three tenets, the more money she will make. The danger lies with those who mix up the fantasy world painted in dating advice materials with the real world. People who make this mistake might be indistinguishable initially from the rest of humanity, but there are many telltale signs that a man you're considering dating believes in the world of dating advice columns more than he does in the one he is living in.

HE THINKS THAT THE FEMALE EQUIVALENT TO BEING A SPORTS FAN IS LIKING SHOES

If you think about it, sports fandom is rather time-consuming and complex. Rarely does a sports fan commit himself (or herself, of course) to following more than two or three sports, because otherwise there'd be no time to sleep or go to work. In any big sport, there are usually professional and college levels to follow during the season and endless off-season opportunities for obsessing over the sport, such as arranging your fantasy team for next season and playing the official video games featuring cartoon versions of your favorite players.

In contrast, shoes usually have three dimensions—do you like them, can you afford them, and do they hurt your feet? Even for women who have cultivated a Carrie Bradshaw level of shoe obsession, the topic is hardly what you'd call mentally straining. (Carrie was far more obsessed with sex, after all.) If you have been bitten by the shoe bug—don't feel guilty if you have, since you are only human—you may one day find yourself spending the sixty seconds it takes to tell the exhaustive tale of going over these three factors before making a shoe purchase. If this happens and your listener says, "Women like to go on about their shoes as much as men like to obsess over sports," you have someone who has mixed up the dating advice world with the real one. This goes doubly if you are prone to pontificating at length on the NFL draft with your friends, which is in no way mutually exclusive from having a mild case of shoe frenzy.

HE THINKS THE FEMALE DEFINITION OF "SENSE OF HUMOR" IS "MAN WHO CRACKS JOKES THAT MAKE HER LAUGH JUST LOUDLY ENOUGH TO BE CUTE AND SHOW OFF HER PRETTY TEETH, BUT NOT SO LOUDLY AS TO DRAW ATTENTION"

Every single bit of dating advice text in the world, especially that aimed at men, makes a big deal out of how every woman wants a man with a sense of humor. Rarely is this trait defined, but that's because it doesn't have to be. In the dating advice world, women have a sense of humor when they laugh at men's jokes and men have a sense of humor when they crack jokes. If you find yourself better than a man at cracking jokes and he accuses you of not having a sense of humor, you've managed to go on a date with someone who has mixed up the dating advice world with yours.

HE THINKS THERE'S NO RELATIONSHIP BETWEEN THE PRESSURE TO BE THIN AND NOT EATING

One of the favorite "Why do women do that?" complaints in dating advice columns is, "Why must women order salads with dinner or pick at their food? I want someone who digs in and eats!" Maybe these people think that a woman who has to have things in her mouth will be casting around desperately for a cock to gobble when she's done eating. Sadly, men who write in to dating advice columns and complain about women who push food around on their plates never add, "And her waist was so tiny; why do women have to be so skinny?"

This disconnect is first-class evidence that dating advice fans don't understand that men and women have very similar bodies, and that women, like men, absorb calories in food and, as with men, if those calories are not expended as energy, they will turn to fat. Or, if men who make this complaint understand that women do metabolize food, perhaps they think that women don't actually need to eat unless men are around, and spend all their nondate time shopping for shoes.

HE EXPRESSES FEAR THAT "INTELLECTUAL" ACTIVITIES WILL CAUSE HIS BALLS TO FALL OFF

In the fantasy world of dating advice columns, the extreme biological differences between men and women cause women's gonads to be excited by "cultural" events, even though those events cause men's gonads to turn gangrenous with a rapidity that resembles what happens to a vampire you shove into the sun. Theater, foreign films, art museums, educational lectures, and libraries are all assumed to be deadly to men and to be avoided at all costs by women who would like to make company with men.

That said, men who buy this line of blooey tend to be dodgy about it, so you may have to prod. If you ask a guy you're dating to go to a museum and he seems to be casting for excuses, say, "Did you know that the vast, vast majority of art in the museum was created by men? Also, did you know that most ballets were written by men? And that most foreign films were directed by men? And that most operas were written by men? And that most of the literature that has made it into the official canon was written by men? And that men still dominate the top levels of college faculty and that most experts consulted by the media are men?"

If you can reach the end of that litany and his head hasn't exploded, then he may just be afraid to run into his ex-girlfriend, the museum curator. Go see an Italian film revival instead. But if your new beau has been damaged by dating advice columns, well, just make sure you have him outside to spiel off these questions so you can hose off your patio after the cognitive dissonance creates an uncontainable amount of internal skull pressure.

HE BELIEVES MEN ARE BIOLOGICALLY UNABLE TO DESIRE MARRIAGE OR CHILDREN

This may cause him some serious mental discomfort, since he might actually be out there carefully reading dating advice columns with the abstract hope that he can convince a woman to marry and have babies with him. But in dating advice materials, there's a lot of humor had at the expense of those desperate women with their inexplicable desires for marriage and babies, so it's clear that proper men recoil at the very idea right up until the day they are possessed by demons and propose.

You can tell you've got one of these on your hands if he's on the lookout for "desperate" statements about marriage you make so that he can demonstrate the proper disdain. If you think that marriage is an unsalvageable patriarchal institution that you'd only join at gunpoint, and you express this opinion to him, he'll only hear the word "marriage" dropping from a woman's lips and assume you're trying to rope him. If this is the case, you'll find out about his freakishness and be able to drop him quickly enough.

Falling short of that, you still have options. Idly mention if you're attending a baby shower or wedding soon. All the better if you can give a quick, condescending roll of the eyes. If he reacts to you as if you'd said, "I like you! So when can you knock me up?" then you know he's a lost cause.

HE EXPECTS THAT YOU'LL PRETEND YOU'RE A VIRGIN

The standard assumption in all dating advice is that men in particular are repulsed at the very thought that women they date may have had prior sexual relationships. The "men and women are completely opposite" thing is a little weaker in this regard, because I haven't seen any dating advice columns that suggest that women love to hear lavish comparisons between themselves and women their dates have slept with in the past, but still, it's assumed that the tendency to get territorial at the mere hint that your date has a past is a man thing.

Thus, women are particularly advised never to mention they have ex-boyfriends, and maybe they want to leave the impression that they haven't ever touched a penis. If they've only been in relationships with women before, though, they don't get a pass, because, if you'll recall, in the dating advice alternate universe, all people are heterosexual.

HE THINKS THAT A WOMAN HAS A BOOTY AND
A MAN SIMPLY HAS BOOTY

Dating advice materials assume pretty straightforwardly that men are in it for the sex and women are in it for the money. That women can obtain jobs and earn their own money now doesn't seem to interfere with this assumption at all. Nor does this view allow for the idea that women might actually want sex for its own sake. Some of the more sexist books and websites even suggest that while men treat women like sex objects, women return the favor by treating men like "success objects." (Which is assumed to make it fair and negate the need for feminism.)

Men who believe this make really bad dates, because they treat dates like transactions. The only way to guard yourself against this is to go dutch on everything. If you allow a man who thinks of dates as transactions to pick up a tab, you'll find out to your dismay that he's running a ledger in his head. Let him buy you a $3 drink? You owe him a lingering hug, possibly a kiss. Let him buy you dinner? You owe him a shot to see nipple. A few dinners in a row buys the strict transaction guy sexual intercourse. The strict transaction mentality can make it distinctly unerotic to participate in anything sexual with these guys, of course. If you let a guy pick up your tab, you may be pleasantly surprised to find out that he's just nice and doesn't approach dating like a transaction, but I wouldn't risk it, at least at first.

HE THINKS THAT "LESBIANS" ARE WOMEN WHO ARE
JUST SO EAGER TO PLEASE MEN THEY'D FUCK THEIR
OWN SISTERS IN FRONT OF THEM

Actually, that's from the "Men Ruined by Porn" section.

Men Who Think You're a "Challenge"

Despite the stereotype that romantic comedies are ruinous solely to women's expectations, the truth of the matter is there are a lot of men out there who have some pretty cracked opinions on what's hot and sexy, opinions that seem to come directly from romantic comedies. One of the most irritating of these is the idea that nothing is more romantic than taming the wild filly. We've all seen this plot in movies—the headstrong, intellectual young woman brought to her senses by the firm guidance of a tough young stud. It's all fun and games until you're a feminist, which is translated as "wild filly who needs taming" in romantic comedy terms. Which means that you're going to find yourself in many situations where men have absorbed the lessons of *The Philadelphia Story* and all its sequels, and are going to try to woo you by taking you down a few notches. So, some strategies on fighting them off.

FIRST, LEARN TO SPOT THEM

Sometimes this isn't hard. My all-time favorite story of someone trying to hit on me with the "fight with them, they love that" strategy involves the guy who caught me drinking a Miller Lite, bought me some microbrew, came over, and said, "I bought that for you so you can learn to drink real beer." However, not all of them are that easy to spot right off the bat, since most have learned to have a little more subterfuge. The rule of thumb is that a guy is enamored of you-as-a-challenge if he seems to think that your habits, tastes, or intellectual pursuits exist only to be analyzed and possibly corrected by men. Mix in the fact that he will be oblivious to hints to buzz off and you'll know you've managed to attract someone who thinks you're a challenge.

For instance, these guys are drawn like flies to women who are reading or writing in public. While it's quite likely true that some women do read or write in public in an attempt to attract men, some of us honestly do have a reason not to be sequestered in the house to read or write. The thinks-you're-a-challenge guy will interrupt you to ask what you're reading or writing, but more importantly, he'll be aggressive in questioning you about it. (I can't blame a decent guy simply looking for an opening, but they tend to be doing just that and nothing more.) To diagnose if he's that kind of guy, I tend to just flash the title of the book at him or answer rather curtly. If he asks a bunch of leading, nosy questions about what it is—"So, you're a big feminist, then?" being the most obnoxious—it's time to run him off. However, as the above beer example shows, some guys-who-think-you're-a-challenge will seek anything to be aggressive about.

WHAT NOT TO DO TO GET RID OF HIM

The number one thing about these guys is that they can't take no for an answer. "No" is a challenge, and remember, they think they want a challenge. "No" will eventually work, if you are very repetitive and show no other signs of life besides the word "no." That can be time-consuming and irritating, though. Trying to escalate the strength of the rejection can make it even worse. Whatever you do, don't try to be clever and say, "Oh, I get it. You're going to tame the wild, overintellectualized feminist beast. Good luck with that." Yes, it's funny, but it's also exactly what the female lead in a romantic comedy would say, and will probably only encourage him.

STRATEGY ONE TO RUN HIM OFF

The key is that these guys only think they want a challenge. What they want is someone who will offer token resistance and then fall into their arms, having learned the danger of their wicked feminist ways. As such, the Chatty Cathy routine works pretty well to run them off. When a guy starts the aggressive questioning, use that as your excuse to run your mouth, not letting him get a word in edgewise, going over every detail of your intellectual world in great detail. If he can't get a word in edgewise, he can't live out his fantasy and will run away soon enough. A good preventive strategy is to be obnoxiously feminist too. Don't just read or tap away on your laptop in public. Do so with an Andrea Dworkin book sitting title-up next to you and a NOW sweatshirt on. Go way over their heads. This might also work as a good filter, since you know anyone who'll chat you up if you look like that doesn't want to change a damn thing about you.

STRATEGY TWO TO RUN HIM OFF

Just don't be a challenge at all. This one might be a little harder to pull off, because it takes a certain Zen lack of ego, but it can work. Every challenging question he asks, simply agree with whatever he's saying and refuse to elaborate. "You're right." "Yeah, probably." "I'm sure whatever .you're saying is true, I wouldn't know." No static, no electricity, nothing to keep him motivated. Much, much harder to pull off than the first one, but it can be amusing if you're good at it.

When You Won't Just Get Cancer and Die

My working theory is that romantic comedies are the work of Satan, and not the good Satan. For one thing, they are universally disdained as "chick flicks," and yet somehow a great number of men absorb the message of the two most odious romantic comedy clichés. The first is the headstrong woman who is tamed by The Cock, as previously mentioned. In these flicks, the woman's headstrongness is shown as brittle, career-oriented, and unromantic about sex. And that's bad enough, but there's an even worse stereotype of the headstrong woman lurking in the annals of romantic-comedy-cum-melodrama, and that's the flighty but headstrong eccentric who teaches the hero a thing or two about life before exiting stage right, often due to some sort of disease. She has to die or leave somehow, because audiences are incapable of picturing the heroine as a wife, since wives are supposed to be submissive and competent.

For what it's worth, the best antidote to this cliché is probably Sofia Coppola's movie *The Virgin Suicides,* where the eccentric, exotic female lead kills her own damn self, leaving the viewer with the uncomfortable impression that being an exotic fantasy who must somehow exit stage right after forever changing some impressionable young man isn't all it's cracked up to be.

My field research for this guide (i.e., asking my feminist friends) indicates that many feminists find that this particular romantic comedy cliché gives them real problems in real life. Many a young man will fall for the headstrong feminist, on the theory that she's the quirky gal who will change his life forever. And then when reality sets in and it turns out that she's not likely to develop leukemia any time soon, things fall apart. There's not much in the way of advice on how to handle that, since those situations tend to self-terminate, but you can jazz it up a little.

FAKE YOUR DEATH

Give him the movie. Consider it a romantic parting gift.

IF HE DUMPS YOU FIRST, ACT REALLY RELIEVED

He won't see it coming, which is death to the movie-trained mentality. If you have trouble feeling relieved, think about how funny it will be when he realizes that you're not going to sob and sob over him, and that might help.

DUMP HIM FIRST AND TELL HIM THAT YOU'RE DATING A REAL BRUISER NAMED HARLEY

Warning: While this is really funny, if you do this, you will be helping create a Nice Guy™, a concept I'll describe in detail later.

TELL HIM TO SAVE THE WORLD

One wrinkle in the whole thing is the lighter version of this cliché, which is the Superhero's Girlfriend. You know the cliché. Superman, Spiderman—they fall in love with headstrong, quirky, awesome, and for once competent women. But you will never see the headstrong girlfriend actually marry the superhero and scare the audience with the idea of a bona fide wife having a mind of her own. Your soon-to-be ex, however, is not a superhero and so can't really give you the speech about how he loves you but alas, he doesn't want to put you in danger by dating you. So, you could, if you wanted to, tell him that you love him but you're holding him back from saving the world. He knows the cliché and may just eat it up.

TELL HIM YOU HAVE TO SAVE THE WORLD

Just recite the superhero's speech to him and blow his mind. It's not supposed to work that way; women aren't the ones who are supposed to begrudgingly give up True Love for duty. True Love is supposed to be their duty.

While he sits there with his mind blown, run away. Don't forget, while fleeing the premises, to leave a sign on his door warning other women that he's been ruined by films where the heroine up and dies, leaving the hero to face the world stronger for having known her and unweakened for having had to pay attention to her.

I pick on antifeminists a lot, but I suppose they're right in one regard—it's totally easy to be a woman. If you go into any grocery store in the country, you can see that women have a big advantage over men in this department, because everywhere you turn, you'll see instruction manuals on the art and science of being a perfect woman. Tons of them, really, all of them coming out monthly and nicely scented by big names like Calvin Klein and Ralph Lauren to improve your reading experience. Men don't have this advantage. Sure, there are some titles for men to compete with all the ones for women, such as *GQ* or *Men's Health,* but on the whole women have a much larger selection of helpful advice on achieving perfection as defined by whoever controls the stinky press.

But buying and reading all those magazines can be both time-consuming and expensive, so for your benefit, I've summarized the major lessons in reaching the women's magazine–defined ideal of feminine perfection.

BE WHITE

You don't even have to read the covers of the magazines to gather this lesson, since the parameters of who gets to be a cover model are enough to convey the message. Simply stated, simply achieved, no? You also need to be able to slice cheese on your hipbones. (Though, for the love of all that is heavily perfumed and glossy, don't actually put the cheese in your mouth!) However, in recent years another option has cropped up—in lieu of being white, you can always be Oprah.

MEMORIZE A LOT OF COMPLEX SEXUAL POSITIONS AND EMPLOY THEM

In the women's magazine world, sex is extremely complicated, and knowing what goes where while doing it takes a great deal of lengthy study, with no hope for a degree at the end, no less. *Cosmo* has a Sex Position of the Week, implying that there are 365 separate ways to place a penis inside a vagina. (Being a Perfect Woman requires you to be straight, of course.) A random one:

> *Your guy lies on his back. Facing him, lower yourself onto his penis in a kneeling position. Keeping your knees on the bed, curl your feet around the inside of his legs, likely around his knees. Lean forward and grab the bedsheets on either side of his head. While holding the sheets—and with your feet wrapped around your man's calves—squeeze your butt, tilt your pelvis and move in small, tight motions.*

Put your feet on the outside of his calves or grab the headboard instead of the sheets, and it's a totally different position, we swear. With this fascinating ability to generate dozens, possibly hundreds, of sex positions, you can dazzle any man. Which you'll need to do.

UNDERSTAND THAT MEN ARE EASILY BORED AND CAN BARELY TAKE AN INTEREST IN WOMEN UNLESS YOU CONSTANTLY DAZZLE THEM

I opened the online women's magazine portal iVillage.com to find the headline "Ten Things Good Girls Can Learn from Porn Stars." This is just one in a continuing series in roughly every women's magazine of twenty tips here, ten tips there, and fifty tips over there on how to accomplish the Sisyphean task of persuading men to take a sexual interest in you enough to want to fuck you. This notion that men require a constant stream of innovative enticements into sex has been disputed by sitcoms, which often argue that men actually like sex, to the point where they will pester women to have sex with them, even if said women are actively busy doing something that's not on a long list of tips to make men interested. We eagerly await a ruling from the Council on Gender Stereotypes to determine which one is true.

A MILD AMOUNT OF DIVERSITY IS OKAY, SO LONG AS YOU DON'T GET ALL CRAZY

The infatuation with quizzes in women's magazines leads one to conclude that there are three, sometimes even four, mild variations of personality that you can have while being a Perfect Woman. From the cover of *O:* "Four Love Types (Don't say another word to him until you take our quiz)." Inside, you find that you get to have one of only four love "types," but once you figure out which one you belong to, you have determined your "mate fate." As you can guess, of the four love types, none are "lesbian separatist" or "curmudgeonly single and happy about it." You are permitted, to varying degrees, to be an Explorer, a Builder, a Negotiator, or a Director. Your intrepid researchers delved into the story and confirmed what we suspected—it's not actually okay to be a Director (described in the article as "grating" and "cold"). But that's three whole mild variations on personality you're permitted to have, and we all know that being able to pick between Diet Coke, Coca-Cola Zero, and Diet Pepsi is the true meaning of freedom.

LEARN HOW TO TAME THE WILD BEAST THAT IS YOUR BODY

The Perfect Woman knows that her body is always trying to undermine her, and she must learn to coax it into submission. Thus, headlines for articles about maintaining your physical appearance read a lot like blurbs on dog-training manuals. From a cover of *Redbook:* "Calm Your Cranky Skin, Thirty-Two Solutions." While we imperfect women may be stuck wondering, "Skin gets cranky?" the Perfect Woman is already on the job, teaching her skin to suck it up and be cheerful and stop being such a drag at the party. If those thirty-two tips on decrankying your skin don't help, you can always call on the Skin Whisperer.

THE BEST WAY TO FIGURE OUT WHAT'S BEST FOR YOU IS TO MONITOR WHAT EVERYONE ELSE IS DOING

In the women's magazine world, there's a carefully cultivated sense that everyone else knows what to do except you, and you need the magazine to find out the big secrets that everyone is keeping from you. In other words, part of being the Perfect Woman is feeling insecure and suspecting everyone is more Perfect than you. *Glamour* lets you know what your sexual desires should be with "What Everybody You Know Is Really Into in Bed." Because without an intricate detailing out of what everyone else wants, how could you possibly know what you want? Of course, there's some reason to suspect nosiness sells more magazines with this headline than anxiety about what's right and proper to want in bed, but the lowly motivations of women not seeking Perfection is beyond the scope of this chapter.

LACK OF TIME IN THE DAY IS NO REASON TO FALL DOWN ON YOUR WOMANLY DUTIES OF COOKING, CLEANING, AND RELENTLESS GROOMING OF YOURSELF

Women's magazines will not let you fall down on the job of being perfectly gorgeous and made up with dinner on the table every night just because you clock in as many hours at work as a man. Every magazine has tons of tips and advice on how to attend to your endless stream of womanly duties in less time than it used to take, because god knows that simply taking a break once in a while from compulsive femininity is out of the question. From *Glamour* hawking "One-Minute Summer Hair and Makeup" to *Redbook* helpfully suggesting, "Dinner? Done. Seven Make-Ahead Meals," you can rest easy knowing that the Perfect Woman can do and have it all with five or even six minutes left in her day for herself.

THE PERFECT WOMAN CHEERFULLY PREPARES FOOD SHE WON'T EAT ON A REGULAR BASIS

Woman's Day might be my favorite magazine in this regard, since every single issue has a big headline about how to lose weight at the top and a smaller one hawking recipes that are *not* in the diet plan just a few lines below. "Lose Ten Pounds in Four Weeks" will be bumped right up next to "Turtle Cheesecake Recipe to Die For." Why make these delicious, fattening foods when you can't eat them because of your endless dieting? Are there legions of women seeking Perfection who serve this week's recipe for four-cheese pasta to everyone else in the house before retiring to the back room to eat a plate of lettuce and whole-grain rice?

HALVING YOUR BODY WEIGHT IS A GOOD WAY TO GET YOUR FIFTEEN MINUTES OF FAME

When this survey was conducted, at least three of the magazines in our sample set (the rack at the grocery store) had women who weighed 50 percent or less than they did before they started their diets. If you can pull off this amazing feat by going from, say, 250 pounds to 125 pounds, you get a magazine cover with all the attendant Photoshopping to make you look especially hot. Be ready to provide a fat photo where you look stoned, stupid, or lonely, and be aware that you'll be asked to pose in a bathing suit. However, almost no one who loses this amount of weight actually reaches the proper levels of emaciation to be a swimsuit model, so don't flinch too hard when they imply that your 125-pound self is still kind of fat by giving you a one-piece swimsuit with a skirt attached.

Warning: Do not try this shortcut to fame if you already weigh 125 pounds, unless you're already a famous socialite and you don't mind being held up as a skeletal horror story by the tabloids.

PERFECT WOMEN BUY ENTIRE OUTFITS

Most women's magazines have a feature where they show off this season's fashions by showing you entire outfits with the price tag for the whole thing, from the shirt to the earrings to the slacks, at the top of the page somewhere. The implication clings to the pages that women should go and buy entire outfits and perhaps put each outfit, accessories and everything, into a dry cleaning bag so they remember to wear everything as one ensemble. Because it's not enough to make you feel bad about your diet, your lack of a fake tan, and your inability to make many pastries you won't eat. You also need to feel insecure about the fact that you buy your clothes haphazardly and, as a consequence, the specter of white pants never enters your wardrobe.

To make it worse, the cheapest of these outfits are generally advertised as "only" $100 or $150. If you feel eligible to leave your house wearing only a $10 band T-shirt, $30 jeans you wear five days out of the week, and ratty sneakers, think again, sister.

PERFECT WOMEN NEVER AGE PAST FORTY

Luckily, if you are forty, magazines will graciously allow that you exist in articles like "Perfect Skin at Twenty, Thirty, Forty" or "How to Be Sexy at Twenty, Thirty, or Forty." If you're wondering about having perfect skin or being sexy at forty-one, you've already failed in your mission. Aging only happens to the weak and unprepared.

MALE DOUCHEBAGGERY SHOULDN'T CAUSE YOU TO FEEL ANYTHING LESS THAN PERFECTLY ENTHUSIASTIC ABOUT LIVING AS IF MEN WERE YOUR SOLE REASON FOR EXISTING

Many, many women's magazines have features called things like "What Men Really Think" or "Real Men Speak Up," and either by accident or design, the real men they seem to find are all tools, leaving the unpleasant sensation that tooldom is a major facet of being a man. From an article on ten annoying things women do (because we're all the same thing) on iVillage.com:

> *They cry over anything: a sad movie (or even a happy one), a broken nail or a haircut gone awry. What's worse, they expect us to clean up the emotional mess. And if there's one thing we suck at, it's dealing with a crying woman on our shoulder.*

Any discerning reader will grasp from this passage that the author posits that all men will immediately—upon discovering you tearing up from being moved by a movie or just frustrated because your painfully broken nail is the last straw in a wretched day—start to back off and make uncomfortable jokes about how your feelings don't count, then hold you responsible for all nasty stereotypes about women's irrationality forevermore. But you, being a Perfect Woman, aren't supposed to stop and wonder why the hell you'd put up with a douchebag like that. Perfect Women appreciate their douchebags, feel grateful to have them, and if they reach upper-level female Perfection, they find sexist douchebaggery aimed at them kind of cute.

Nice Guys

Some of the more honest of us admit that we all, male and female alike, have a tendency toward Nice Guy thought. The term "Nice Guy" is a bit confusing, because Nice Guys are not actually very nice, but it's the preferred term because that's invariably how such guys describe themselves. Nice Guys come in many shapes and sizes, but here are the basic traits that define the Nice Guy.

1. The belief that he personally is what every woman should want in a man, which is Niceness. What makes him Nice is pretty vague at times. Some Nice Guys are Nice because they have jobs, some because they won't cheat, some because they will remember your birthday, and some because they really don't think they'd hit a woman.

2. However, despite possessing the quality of Niceness that other folks consider basic decency, the Nice Guy is not getting the dates or sex he thinks he is entitled to. That he feels entitled to these things is not considered evidence that he's not really that Nice.

3. That he is not getting these dates must mean that women in general have a severe lack of good judgment. Well, at least the women he wants to date do.

Women are often described as shallow, infatuated with jerks, and materialistic. Skinny blondes with big breasts in particular will be held up as examples of women who need to look beyond surface appearances when seeking dates and give their surface appearance over to the Nice Guys in exchange for the Nice Guys being so very Nice.

4. Since women seem to like jerks so very much, the Nice Guy is going to morph into one any day now and start reaping the pussy that he's entitled to. This hypothetical transition to jerkdom is usually planned for a near future that doesn't seem likely to manifest anytime soon. It never occurs to the Nice Guy that he is already a jerk if his supposed niceness is contingent on getting laid.

There are various flavors of Nice Guys. the hardest one to avoid is your male friend who hangs around expecting you to start dating him without ever telling you what he wants. In this situation, you usually only find out he was infatuated with you when you start dating someone else and he blows his lid at you, accusing you of passing him over.

If he's got a particularly bad case of Nice Guy fever, he may only lose his cool after watching you date a series of guys. If you pay close attention, you'll probably find that he's dropping subtle hints the whole time that he's being a pining Nice Guy. If you have a male friend saying things like, "I'm concerned that this new guy you're seeing, the one who fosters puppies in his free time when he's not at work helping orphans, might be an asshole," just ask him outright if he's harboring a crush on you. He may not appreciate finding out for certain that you're not going to date him, but at least you've given him a reason to stop pining, or at least to pine for someone else.

If you're friends with a Nice Guy who isn't pining for you, then you'll know for certain, because he'll talk nonstop about the women he does crush on, usually about how they have terrible taste in men and need to drop the current jerk for him. Having a Nice Guy friend will frustrate you, because it's only a matter of time before he extrapolates his current crush's supposed bad taste in men to all women everywhere, with some variation on the Nice Guy lament, "Why won't women date Nice Guys like me?"

At this point, whatever you do, no matter even if you have a giant crush on your Nice Guy friend, do not say, "Well, I'd date you." If you do this, you will find out that he excludes you from the category "all women" for reasons you probably don't want to know. It could be that he doesn't consider you a woman because you're easy to talk to, but it could be that he doesn't really consider you a woman because you're a feminist or because you prefer jeans to skirts or because you don't make it a habit of dating jerks that he can loathe.

In the worst cases, Nice Guys can slip into racist, imperialist fantasizing about foreign women who have nice, poverty-lowered standards in what they'll put up with from a guy. It's never phrased that way, of course. It's usually something about how women "over there" know how to treat a man, unlike the stuck-up bitches in America. Once a Nice Guy has slid into racist fetishizing, he is usually unsalvageable. The best thing you can do is wait until he brings home potential mail-order brides from Russia and slips them pamphlets explaining how to get a green card outside of marrying a Nice Guy.

But there is still hope for men with a minor case of Nice Guyism. All they need to really do is take to heart the notion that women have as much right as men to have sex with someone for their own reasons, and not as a cookie that's handed out for good behavior. Outside of this sense of entitlement, Nice Guys can often have many good qualities that make them worthy friends. I have many male friends who have successfully recovered from their Nice Guy tendencies by reminding themselves of this every time the urge to get bitter creeps in.

Whatever you do, *do not pity-fuck a Nice Guy*. Not even if you make it clear to him beforehand that you're acting out of boredom, pity, and horniness. You're just hurting his chances at recovery by making him feel that he's going to get laid by lurking around feeling sorry for himself. He's not going to improve until he learns to quit treating women like vagina-vending machines that cough up the goodies when you make a standardized payment. "One pretending to care about her feelings, one door opening, one dinner purchased, I get sex now." The longer he thinks like this, perversely, the harder it will be for him to be charming enough to get women to sleep with him because they want to. So do your Nice Guy friends a favor and refuse to fuck them unless they have genuinely learned to charm your pants off. Trying to your pants off is not charming.

Even if you're in love with your Nice Guy friend and he suddenly decides to love you back, you may want to avoid dating him until he recovers from his Nice Guy tendencies. Nice Guys put women on pedestals, and actually dating someone is not conducive to keeping her on a pedestal. After all, when you spend a lot of time around someone, her faults start seeping out. Maybe you're clumsy. Maybe you belch. Maybe you're absentminded. Whatever your minor imperfections are, they will seem glaring and odious to your Nice Guy. Once you fall off that pedestal, he'll be picking on you all the time, so just avoid the situation completely.

If he starts carrying on about what "all women" do, remind your Nice Guy friend that "all women" is a category that includes his sainted mother and indeed his grandmother as well. Tough love might be required in these circumstances. Your Nice Guy friend may not want to hear that his male rivals are often good guys, but if they are, he needs to hear it. Not until he embraces reality will he start his path to recovery.

ARE THERE NICE GIRLS?

Are there women who moan and groan about how "all men" (or women, if she's a lesbian), or at least the ones she wants, are perfect in every way except for their bad taste in women? Are there women who blame their lack of success in the dating world on a puzzling lack of appreciation for Niceness in the objects of their desire? Yes, though their numbers are minor compared to the number of men who are

Nice Guys. Thanks to the patriarchy, most women are adept at blaming themselves for being unattractive, even inventing flaws that don't actually exist when coming up with reasons that men may not want to date them.

In pop culture, at least, both Nice Girls and Nice Guys hold women responsible for their problems. Nice Guys want women to quit choosing "jerks"—i.e., guys who are not them. However, Nice Girls will actually suggest that their romantic rivals should let the men they want go, so the Nice Girls can have them. See: Dolly Parton's "Jolene" and Avril Lavigne's "Girlfriend."

Whither Cats?

In early 2007, the *New York Times* published a story on the fact that a slight majority of adult women in America now live without a husband, quite possibly for the first time in American history. This is mostly true due to relatively uninteresting demographic trends. Women on average live longer than men, so there are more widows than widowers. Add to that the relative acceptability of divorce, growing acceptance of open lesbianism, and the fact that women tend to put off marriage until a little later in life, and you have your reasons that a slight majority of adult women are living without a husband in the house. It should have been nonthreatening, but most antifeminist types got no further than the words "majority," "women," "without," and "husbands," and panic ensued. In their eyes, it was bad enough that women were running around without male keepers, but now that we singletons were the majority, it was a sign of the end times. Despite the fact that "without husband" meant everything from being widowed to cohabitating to having a husband overseas fighting the war, it was assumed that the number of single women was high because of legions of high-heeled hot mamas who refuse to wear white because it's not their color.

As such, the antifeminist cry was heard from coast to coast, from the Internet to your "concerned" relatives pressuring you to find a man to settle down with: "CATS!"

Why the fluffy, beclawed favored pet of yardless people has become the primary symbol of stubborn unwillingness to submit to male authority is anyone's guess. Some people reference the association of cats and witches, and some argue that it's more mundane, that people link cats and single women because single women are somewhat less likely than married women to have the big yards and suburban homes where dogs roam. Some suggest that a cat's notorious stubborn streak is equated with the supposed stubbornness that single women must have if they are resisting marriage. Regardless of the reason, women are told, over and over, that if they don't get married as soon as possible to anyone who will have them, cats are in their future.

SAMPLES

• From Tom Purcell on January 26, 2007: "And when you hear a prowler rattling the door knob in the middle of the night, whom do you send to investigate? Your cat?"
• From Mary Graber on the same day: "According to the *Times*, women are now living with their cats and lovin' it!"
• And so on and so forth.

The premise of the cat threat is confusing. Are women supposed to be so afraid of sharing their living quarters with a cat that they drop whatever they're doing and get married immediately? Is there something so intrinsically awful about cats that this is supposed to scare us? If single women are so stubborn about maintaining our space that we refuse to share it with men, why would we then cave to live with creatures that are supposedly so awful that the very mention of them is supposed to leave us quaking in fear?

And do men never own cats? Have people who whip out the cat threat never seen Robert De Niro coddling his pet cat in *Meet the Parents*?

My theory on why the cat threat continues to be used by antifeminists, despite the fact that it doesn't really make any sense, is that it still has the power to make women defensive. There is a sliver of truth to it, in that there are a lot of people who have pet cats and many of them are single women. People's first urge when confronted with a stereotype is to try to prove it's not true, so the single-women-with-cats thing is attractive because there are so many examples of how it is true.

That said, the people who wield the battle cry "CATS!" don't really bother to make the case as to why a single-woman-with-cats is a *bad* thing, so that's where to deal with them. And I don't mean ask people to tell you why they dislike cats, because cat haters are uniformly able to cough a million unfair reasons for their sick prejudices. (I have cats, in case you can't tell.) But I suggest looking at the implicit argument behind the stereotype, which is that in the supposed battle between cats and men, it's a tragedy if cats win the spot as your bedmate and life companion.

This is all setting aside for a moment that a lot of beds feature a man, a woman, and a cat or two. What else was the king-size invented for?

See, in the battle between Husband and Cats, the case is never really made for husbands. We just assume that they're better, but why? If husbands stink up the bathroom, you can't fix the problem immediately by cleaning their box. Husbands might have furry bellies, but they don't purr when you scratch them. And cats never pout and declare that you don't really love them if you don't change your name to Mrs. Cat.

If you're single and people taunt you with the cat thing, it might be wise to point out that they have the burden of proof on them to demonstrate (1) that cats are somehow antihusband and (2) assuming #1 is true, that husbands are better than cats.

The best part is that almost no one who makes tired jokes about single women having cats even has the nerve to bring up The Cock as a major point in the favor of husbands. It's the downside to being old-fashioned.

If worse comes to worst, you can always mention that no one on *Sex and the City* owned a cat. Since *Sex and the City* is the touchstone of all antifeminist rants against single women—or at least the only one outside of accusing us of having cats—the cognitive dissonance of pointing this out will, at bare minimum, buy you enough time to escape the conversation gracefully.

So You Wanna
Buy a Vibrator

Y ou're a big girl now and your pillow-humping days are over. You want a vibrator. What to do next should be easy: Go to the sex shop, select your purchase, give the nice lady at the register her money, and get your new toy back in a brown paper bag. Sure, it works that way in the lands of Sodom and Gomorrah, otherwise known as San Francisco and New York City. In the red states it can be a little more complicated than that.

In 2003, housewife and Southern Baptist Joanne Webb was arrested in Burleson, Texas, for violating a Texas law banning the sale of dildos. She sold the sex toys like a good housewife should, at Tupperware-style parties that were generally promoted as a way to spice up your Jesus-approved marital boudoir. That this was a godly operation didn't stop the law from interfering, however, because while Jesus may approve of your nine-inch vibrating dildo, state legislators who feel mildly inadequate when faced with such a device most decidedly do not. As of now, the Supreme Court has decided that sex toys are beneath its attention and the law still stands in Texas.

So where does this leave you, the sex toy consumer? You have a number of options:

PURCHASE YOUR TOYS IN THE MAIL
In a sense, this serves the assholes who banned dildo sales right, because it's direct evidence that banning sex toys only helps enrich the ungodly masturbators in the

blue states while sending money out of the red states. It also appeals to a sense of history, since buying everything you could ever need from a catalog is a long-standing rural American tradition. I live in an actual city with shops now instead of out in the middle of nowhere like I used to, but I still do most of my shopping from catalogs out of habit. It's a good option but it does have drawbacks. It's hard to gauge size and texture and battery power from a catalog picture, after all.

GO WITHOUT

I had to include this option by the Liberal Law of Inclusiveness, which states that we are to acknowledge and support all sexual choices that harm no one and involve consenting adults. Now that we've gotten the caveat out of the way, let me remind you that if you do not own a drawerful of brightly colored, scandalous, vibrating objects, then you're only demonstrating that the laws work to the anxiety-ridden sex haters who populate the state legislatures of the South. Also, going without sort of contradicts the entire premise of the "So You Wanna Buy a Vibrator" chapter.

PURCHASE YOUR TOYS AT A LOCAL SEX SHOP

If you live in a more urban area, there might actually be a sex shop that sells vibrators and dildos despite the law. You will quickly learn, however, that in order to purchase them you have to sign a bunch of paperwork clarifying that you are only buying the toys to demonstrate how to put on condoms or some other such nonsexual use. They are not selling you a sex toy, you see. They are selling you an educational model. Personally speaking, I have no ethical quandaries with signing such a thing, since I figure that all uses I or anyone could think of for such toys would be educational to somebody.

PURCHASE YOUR TOYS AT A HOUSE PARTY

If you live in a rural area, this might be your only other option besides online catalogs. As Joanne Webb's example shows, there are often a lot of housewives who don't want to be constrained to selling Tupperware and have branched out into the sex toy department. Her example also shows that this option might be overlaid with a layer of paranoia. Unless you can somehow convince the saleslady that you're really just participating in the demonstration when you frisk her for wires, you might find yourself in a situation where you have to trust in Jesus that the law won't nab you for the crime of wanting sex outside of the prying eyes of Bible-thumpers. Just remember, in most places it's illegal to sell sex toys, but not to buy them.

Part 4.

THE UGLIEST SIDE OF THE BACKLASH: FUNDAMENTALISTS AND ANTICHOICERS

How You Can Tell You're in an Abstinence-Only Classroom

bstinence-only education is an oxymoronic concept. The idea behind it is that instead of giving students sex education, where they learn about sex, contraception, and disease prevention, we refuse to educate them and instead tell them to zip it up and save it for marriage. If the name of this theory were more accurate, it would be called abstinence-only noneducation, because the entire point of it is to withhold information, to refuse to educate.

Proponents of abstinence-only education realized that not educating people and calling it education might raise a few eyebrows, however, so they've devised a number of ways to make not educating students resemble education closely enough to trick people who aren't paying attention, such as school board members. They've devised an entire curriculum of activities and readings that look like education without the education component. Despite this disguise, there are a number of telltale signs that the class you're in is not about education so much as it's about abstinence-only noneducation.

THE LICKING AND THE SUCKING

The Abstinence Clearinghouse, your home for abstinence-only education materials, sells lollipops to pass out to classrooms that say SAVE SEX FOR MARRIAGE. Because few things will make a classroom full of kids think about the importance of avoiding lust like filling the silence of the classroom with the sounds of enthusiastic licking and sucking.

THE SWAPPING SPIT

As reported by Marc Fisher in the February 15, 2007, *Washington Post*, Montgomery County parents discovered that their kids were being taught the basics of not fucking with a little game where kids were given pieces of gum to chew and then instructed, after the chewing had commenced, to swap pieces of gum. The lesson was that if you have sex with someone, you become a chewed-up piece of gum more suitable for throwing on the sidewalk than ever being touched by another person. Granted, that's not quite how the instructors put it, but it's the take-home message from being told, roughly, "You wouldn't want a piece of gum that someone else has chewed, would you?"

That or they were trying to mislead the students about the mechanics of sex. With all the misinformation being touted in abstinence-only classrooms, they might as well just outright tell the girls that having sex leaves your vagina chewed up like a wad of gum.

THE SWEET LITTLE LIES

A report commissioned by Representative Henry Waxman's office in 2004 showed that many abstinence-only textbooks tell more lies than a lover who's cheating on you. Lies discovered in various textbooks include the false statistic that half of gay teenagers have HIV and the made-up theory that abortion causes depression and suicide. But by far the favorite lie of abstinence-only textbooks is also the favorite lie of unfaithful lovers—"No, baby, we don't need to use a condom." Granted, the difference is your lying lover is telling you wrongly there's no risk of disease, and abstinence-only books wrongly state that condoms don't work, but the result is the same: Innocent people are misled into not protecting themselves against disease.

THE ROLE-PLAYING

The Waxman report also found that many of the textbooks peddled tired sexist stereotypes about how boys have all the sexual desire and girls have all the responsibility for saying no. And for those girls who don't find that they enjoy playing little teasing role-playing games with boys, there's strong pressure to do so. One textbook from the *Choosing the Best* series had a story in it where girls were instructed to be passive and never outdo boys in any competition: a story of a princess who gets rejected by the prince after showing him how to slay dragons. If you find yourself in a classroom where you're being instructed in the erotic art of playing at helplessness, it's probably abstinence-only.

THE INSTRUCTOR HAS GIVEN HERSELF A SEXY NICKNAME

In most classes, the teachers go by regular old names like Mr. Stevens or Ms. Williams. Abstinence-only instructors, however, have been known to prefer stage names, much like strippers only without as much class. For example, as reported in the *Dallas Morning News* in March 2007, a local antichoice activist and abstinence-only "educator" named Jennifer Waters volunteers under the moniker "the Sex Lady" to give talks in various high schools about what a terrible thing having sex is. She doesn't yet show up to talk down sex while wearing a miniskirted nun's costume with thigh-highs and garters, but perhaps she'll start after learning how such costumes are even more effective than her nickname at getting kids' minds off the dirty stuff.

THE BONDAGE GAMES AND THE SADOMASOCHISM

The same Miss Waters who calls herself the Sex Lady plays a little game with her students that wouldn't be out of place in a bondage club. She slaps a piece of tape on a student's arm and rips it off to show how having sex with someone makes them stick painfully to you. Supposedly, the sadistic lift of yanking tape off a teenage boy's arm and making him wince in pain is merely an unfortunate side effect for the not-at-all-repressed twenty-six-year-old virgin. She then bounces around the classroom sticking the tape on various students to show that the more sex you have, the less sticky you are. Overcoming codependence is considered a negative thing in the abstinence-only world.

The tape demonstration has nothing, however, on the bit of sadism performed by Christian comedian and abstinence-only educator Keith Deltano, as reported in March 2007 in the *Washington Post.* As part of his show, Deltano has a teenage boy lie down on a table and then holds a cinderblock over the boy's crotch. So far, Deltano has managed to keep his sadistic glee at seeing the terror in his students' eyes at a level low enough that he hasn't yet dropped the cinderblock, but some people fear it's just a matter of time. The excuse for having this demonstration is that he has to show that condoms don't work (on the deadly side of the sweet little lies), but the visual impact of dangling a cinderblock over a teenager's genitals tends to wipe out any interpretations other than the obvious one.

So far, no abstinence-only instructors who prefer to play at being a bottom in the classroom have been found, but with the amount of sexual repression that pours out in your average abstinence-only classroom, it's just a matter of time before one crops up.

In 2005, atrocious R&B singer Nick Cannon released a maudlin song called "Can I Live," accompanied by an even more maudlin video where he assumes the role of the ghost of himself following his mother around while she's pregnant with him and considering an abortion. Cannon unsubtly takes credit for his mother's decision not to abort her pregnancy by showing his ghost self berating her until she gives in and gives birth to him. Apparently, the song is an attempt to convince the audience that it would have been a terrible thing if Cannon's mother hadn't listened to her omnipotent unborn son's pleas, but if you have to sit through the entire video, it's as likely as not to shore up your support for abortion rights, particularly the abortion rights of women gestating impossibly corny R&B singers.

The song was a huge hit on MTV's *Total Request Live,* which shouldn't really be cause for pro-choice concern. After all, the vast majority of the people who voted for the song have probably since gone through puberty, started high school, and moved on past the "sex is icky" stage, a process that can cause someone to reconsider his or her belief that you should be punished with forced childbirth every time you fornicate.

What is cause for concern is that Nick Cannon is not alone. Antichoicers are generally fond of personalizing the fetus at the expense of the pregnant woman, and the more schmaltz involved, the better. From movies like *Silent Scream* to pictures of supposed fetal feet adorning checks to Christian cartoons that star fetuses that can walk and talk, unencumbered by the womb, an entire industry has sprung up of products purporting that fetuses are these entirely separate beings that have no meaningful relationship to pregnant women.

But songs with singing fetuses taking over the narrative voice are something special. The fetus is the perfect cipher for a singer's most reactionary and misogynist politics; after all, it's not like fetuses are going to stand up for themselves and deny that they strongly support antifeminist politics. As such, many male singers have been drawn by the siren's song of passing off some pretty sexist sentiments as fetal opinions.

Seals and Crofts kicked off the canon of singing-for-the-fetus songs with "Unborn Child," though they technically don't cast themselves as the fetus himself so much as they do as his grown male advocates. They rushed the song out in 1974, as if they knew there would be an onslaught of singing fetus songs and they had to get in the first. Since then, there have been countless songs, maudlin to the last, where fetuses express sexist sentiments toward their would-be mothers. Still, antichoice singers haven't really tapped the full potential of using fetuses as ciphers for their reactionary politics, and have limited the political opinions of their imaginary fetal narrators to antiabortion opinions, in songs with titles like "Deliver Me," "Diary of an Unborn Child," and "See No Evil" (the last one from a heavy metal band called Holy Soldier). It's not surprising that antichoicers have a limited imagination when it comes to words they could put in fetal mouths, but I came up with a list of title possibilities for an entire singing fetus album, which could be the comeback career move for a band like Creed.

TIMMY THE SINGING FETUS SINGS SONGS TO SOMEONE'S MOTHER

- "Why Did You Wear That If You Didn't Want to Get Raped?"
- "I'll Grow Up to Be a Criminal If You Divorce Daddy"

- "Women in Other Countries Have It Worse"
- "Your Rights Offend My Religion So They'll Simply Have to Go"
- "Don't Be a Cock-Tease"
- "Don't Call Yourself a Victim Just Because You're a Victim"
- "Housework Is Good for a Pregnant Woman's Waistline"
- "Rape Should Be Legal Because Women Lie"
- "Shoulda Kept Your Legs Shut, Mom"
- "Women Only Want Men for Their Money"
- "Have Me or the Illegal Immigrants Will Take Over"
- "You Can Get Plan B at the Next Hospital"
- "Women Make Less Because They're Lazy"
- "Child Support Is Highway Robbery"
- "Sex Is Icky So That's What You Get"

The last one could totally dominate *Total Request Live* for at least two weeks. Anxious PTAs around the country would eat it up.

Quiverfull

The logical conclusion of the anticontraception, antiabortion wingnut thinking, where women are nothing more than walking uteruses begging to be filled and refilled, comes to fruition in the Quiverfull movement. Yes, they spell it that way, and no, it doesn't appear to be done to make people grate their teeth, though more research is needed. Quiverfull appears to have started because some Protestants envied the supposed Catholic ability to beat women into thorough submission through repeated childbirth. From the way that Quiverfull men tend to strut around like roosters, there also seems to have been some envy of the virile reputation Catholics have in circles that believe all Catholics are Mary-worshipping idolators who are going to hell but are having a lot of sex on the way.

The movement disdains any birth control at all, even using the rhythm method, in no small part because avoiding sex at certain periods of time makes God horny and irritable. Or the husband. It's hard to tell, because Quiverfull types tend to mix up "God" and "husband" quite a bit. For example, the blogger Shakespeare's Sister blogged about a sign she saw in a dry cleaner's that said Moms Are God's Babysitters, which is fairly typical of the treacly slogans that send Quiverfullers and similar wingnuts into raptures. But since the actual day-to-day work of babysitting is done at the financial behest not of God but of husband, it's hard not to imagine that the sign subtly implies that your snoring lump of bathroom-hogging, all-too-human husband should be regarded as the god of your life.

Still, the Quiverfull movement exists outside the mainstream. That said, they aren't that far out of the mainstream, considering how much they have in common with more mainstream conservatism. Take your typical antichoicer, make the subtext of male anxiety about the emasculating nature of contraception really obvious, add some homeschooling, and you've got the Quiverfulls. The various ways that Quiverfulls are like regular wingnuts, only more so, are too numerous to be discounted.

THE BIZARRE NOTION THAT WHAT THE WORLD REALLY NEEDS IS MORE WHITE PEOPLE

The most favored phallic imagery in the Quiverfull movement is the image of an archer shooting child-bows into the world. As Kathryn Joyce, writing for a November 2006 edition of the *Nation*, noted, Quiverfull followers tend to be obsessed with the idea that they've been chosen by God to pump out one baby after another to be warriors for Christianity. And by "Christianity," they mean "white people." Joyce documented the obsession among followers with keep track of following the population trends in countries where any group, from Muslims to Latinos, is becoming a bigger percentage of the population.

The fear that brown hordes are pouring over the border and can only be stopped by white people ferociously procreating hardly sticks to the outskirts of wingnuttery, but is the major selling point for shows like *The O'Reilly Factor* and Lou Dobbs's entire career as of late. It's a little more subtle, of course. Bill O'Reilly prefers to scream about the brown hordes and let the audience draw the implications themselves. When in doubt, racists can always bring up the specter of a pregnant Mexican national swimming across the border to give birth on the American side and have an "anchor baby."

And then there are a few mainstream conservatives who find hinting around tedious and get straight to the point, understanding full well that a good half of their audience doesn't have the mental acuity to draw inferences too well. Mark

Steyn, writing for the *Chicago Sun-Times* in November of 2006, got straight to the point—Scarlett Johansson needs to understand that her pale complexion obliges her to start procreating early and often. After scaring his audience with a story of a Palestinian woman who started procreating at twelve and didn't stop until she had eight live babies, he proceeds to whine that Scarlett Johansson is too busy using condoms to have babies, having wasted ten years already.

> *In a bit of light Bush-bashing the other day, she attacked the president for his opposition to "sex education." If he had his way, she said, "every woman would have six children and we wouldn't be able to have abortions." Whereas Scarlett is so "socially aware" (as she puts it) she gets tested for HIV twice a year.*
>
> *Well, yes. If "sex education" is about knowing which concrete condom is less likely to disintegrate during the livelier forms of penetrative intercourse, then getting an AIDS test every few months may well be a sign that you're a Ph.D. (Doctor of Phenomenal horniness). But, if "sex education" means an understanding of sexuality as anything other than an act of transient self-expression, then Scarlett is talking through that famously cute butt.*

What the Quiverfulls and the mainstream conservatives neglect to do on a regular basis, when trying to raise fears about the world's average skin color browning a couple shades, is to argue for why anyone should give a shit. Hard as it may seem for them to understand, most of us who like our sheets a little less pointy don't really see why it matters what skin color gets the biggest slice of the pie chart.

Appeals to the grandeur of "Western civilization" from Shakespeare to Einstein usually substitute for real arguments in favor of fetishizing whiteness, but anyone who's witnessed the transcendent beauty that is *Baywatch* can probably quarrel with the idea that white people have a universally positive effect on the culture.

YOU CAN HAVE A UTERUS OR BE A FULL-BLOWN ADULT HUMAN BEING, BUT NOT BOTH AT ONCE

Quiverfulls demonstrate a refreshing honesty about their view of women as brood mares. In her *Nation* article, Joyce quoted Jan Hess, the author of the most popular book promoting the movement, as saying, "Our bodies are meant to be a living sacrifice." The "Quiverfaq" online addresses the objection of a woman who doesn't want to wear her body out with constant pregnancy: "There are many very good Biblical reasons that she doesn't 'get to call the shots.' Our generation has absorbed the feminist rhetoric of 'my body, my choice,' forgetting that our bodies are the Lord's, to be used to His glory, and that wives are to be subject to their husbands and under their authority." Your body belongs to God and your husband, and the only use they can find for it is sexual release and baby release.

To be fair, Quiverfulls find women useful for wiping butts and washing clothes, as well. The most famous Quiverfull family in the nation, the Duggars, had their own reality show where Americans could get a full eyeball of the butt-wiping-laundry-doing duty load for Mrs. Duggar. Many viewers ended up wondering how she found time in the day in between wiping butts and washing clothes to make even more babies.

Much as I'd like to assure anyone that this view of women as ambulatory uteruses falls far outside the mainstream, the evidence suggests otherwise. After all, the Supreme Court, which was considered mainstream last I checked, ruled in favor of the federal late-term abortion ban, with Justice Kennedy suggesting in the majority opinion that women who get abortions to save their own lives or health will regret going against their nature, which is ruled completely by uterine productivity. He argued in the opinion against abortion by stating that "respect for human life finds an ultimate expression in the bond of love the mother has for her child."

The woman is her uterus, and uteruses are meant to reproduce by nature. Interests outside of bearing more and more children (including the interest in staying alive despite a difficult pregnancy) do not compute.

In the mainstream media, you see this view as well, with Dean Barnett, writing for the *Boston Globe* on May 21, 2007, discussing how simple the antichoice position is. His editorial was noteworthy not just for its intellectual vapidity, but also for his thoroughness—in an entire op-ed about women's health-care, he did not use the word "woman," "women," or "pregnant" even once. He used the noun "pregnancy," though, leaving the distinct impression that he thinks that pregnancies exist all on their own and have no bearing on the bodies of real human beings.

SELECTIVE OPPOSITION TO MODERNISM

Quiverfulls reject birth control, even the rhythm method, as unnatural, positing instead that the natural order of things is for the god-husband to hump to his heart's content and what body-changing pregnancies that result are just a matter of course. Hysterical Luddite reactions to the sci-fi horrors of the birth control pill and the condom generously pepper Quiverfull literature. From the No Room for Contraception site:

> Society has a lust affair with birth control to the point of not being able to think outside of the box. We live in a contraception "matrix" where it's impossible to believe that there are any harmful effects on marriage, society, and the health of women. This "contraception deception" is the primary force behind the attacks against the contra-contraception message.
>
> For the most part, society doesn't want to hear the message. This message is that, in our culture, contraception leads to increases in abortion, teenage sex, affairs (and subsequent divorce), health problems, and statutory rape.

For people who claim to oppose lust so much, they have a way with breathlessly written literature. Sublimated sexual urges, most likely. The arguments for how contraception somehow increases abortions by reducing unwanted pregnancies are a first-class example of how to craft an argument with zero relationship to the real world. Many anti–birth control activists liken the birth control pill to "pesticide," hoping to link people's discomfort with ingesting toxic chemicals with the horrors of taking a break from being pregnant all the time.

All this suspicion against the miracles of modern medicine is suspiciously absent when addressing the miracles of modern medicine that allow you to bear six, ten, or eighteen children without dying or having your uterus just fall right out of your body from the stress. When it comes to making sure the uterus is in good working order and able to keep producing, technology loses all its sci-fi scariness and instead becomes a good thing. This approach to traditionalism is nothing new to Quiverfullism, though. They cribbed the selective adherence to their own traditionalist ideology from the larger movement in general.

Libertarianism especially has the art of pick-and-choose politics down, with your average libertarian decrying the horrific modern practice of taxing the public to pay for pubic services, in between bounds of driving on publicly funded roads and sending his kids to publicly funded schools. Or, closer to the Quiverfulls on the batshit-crazy scale, you have people adamantly refusing to accept the theory of evolution while only too happy to avail themselves of life- and health-preserving medical treatments that were developed using the theory. It's a tad tough to swallow the idea that we should submit to conservative dictates on how to live when they can't submit to their own ideologies themselves.

Dealing with Street Preachers Holding Forth on the Evils of Fornication

Street preachers are a breed that shows up often in the intersections of a feminist's life in the red states. After all, they are drawn to areas where they assume disobedient females will be plentiful, such as college campuses or places where they suspect "career" women will be walking around. Often, they're right on that count, which may be the first and last time that they can lay claim to accuracy. They're generally identifiable by their weird affection for wearing suspenders, even in hot weather, and they're also usually waving signs that have helpful illustrations of hell on them, so that passing sinners have a good idea what to expect. What's not quite certain is what they expect to accomplish by standing on street corners, holding forth on the evils of fornication and sodomy. Has there ever been a street preacher in the whole history of the art form who has managed to convert a sinner and get her to repent her humping ways? Probably not, so unless they're all holding on to that thin sliver of a hope that they'll be the first, odds are they're out there just to feel superior to people.

Your options:

IGNORE THEM

Generally the best option, for time-management reasons more than anything. Women almost never, ever confront street preachers, though, so it might be worth it to say something to them just to change things up a bit.

ARGUE WITH THEM

If you know anything about the Bible, this can be a lot of fun. I've made a Bible-thumper or two splutter by asking them, if they're so hell-bent on following the antisodomy laws in Leviticus, why they're wearing polyester/cotton blends or shaving their beards off. (I refrain from mentioning menstrual huts, since many of them would probably sign on to a return to that tradition.) You won't change their minds, but making them feel stupid is often worth it.

Whatever you do, if you must argue with a Bible-thumper, don't try to bring the non-Bible reality into things. You might as well be yelling at them in Spanish, for all that they'll understand arguments from reality instead of from their book.

OFFER TO FUCK THEM

Risky proposition, but possibly worth it. Just get the preacher's attention and proposition him. You might want to suggest that it be an even exchange, the sex for the shutting up. As soon as he goes for it, make a big fuss over what a hypocrite he is.

Make sure to have your mace on hand if you should try this strategy. Don't bother with it if you can't get an audience; you're looking for maximum humiliation.

Abortion Is an Industry: Antichoice Myths

If it's not already obvious, I'm a big fan of going out there and tussling with antichoicers. It's tempting, but counterproductive, to ignore them. Antichoicers are like villains out of a comic book, and the more they fester out of sight, the stronger and more insane they become. The reason that they grow stronger out of sight has much to do with the structure of the antichoice movement. The movement is composed of two groups of people: the leaders, who are mostly sadistic misogynists, and the followers, who are sentimental, ignorant nitwits. The leaders devise various ways to use government power to control and harm women, and they gain their strength by telling their followers that it's all about loving babies.

But the myth about loving babies doesn't do enough to sustain the brigades of nitwitted antichoice foot soldiers. Quelling your rational fears that you're in it to hurt women takes serious levels of denial, and that denial won't be fed with sentimental pictures of teeny baby feet alone. Over the years, an entire mythology about abortion has sprung up to justify the antichoice position. Here are some of the major myths, though new ones pop up all the time:

ABORTIONISTS ARE IN IT FOR THE TRUCKLOADS OF CASH

Go to any random antichoice website and you'll see references to the "abortion industry," which is somehow separate in antichoicers' minds from the general "industry" of practicing medicine. The theory about this abortion industry is that unscrupulous, money-hungry doctors convince women to terminate unwanted pregnancies in order to rake in those $500-a-pop abortion fees. Without a huge feminist-driven marketing scheme to convince women to have abortions, the theory goes, women would happily accept every unwanted pregnancy without complaint.

The premise that women are, as a rule, stupid and easily manipulated and don't know their own minds is a constant theme in antichoice literature.

The "abortion industry" myth is so central to the antichoice movement that it even popped up in the evangelical-propaganda *Left Behind* series (as documented by Fred Clark at the blog Slacktivist). The authors introduce the myth through a conversation between a slow-witted but sexy woman and her exasperated but naturally far smarter male friend.

> " . . . *my sister and her bosses and the rest of the staff are out of work now until people start getting pregnant again.*"
>
> "*I get it. It's a money thing.*"
>
> "*They have to work. They have expenses and families.*"
>
> "*And aside from abortion counseling and abortions, they have nothing to do?*"
>
> "*Nothing. Isn't that awful? I mean, whatever happened put my sister and a lot of people like her out of business, and nobody really knows yet whether anyone will be able to get pregnant again.*"

It's hard to believe that antichoicers believe so fervently, despite the self-evident silliness of the belief, that ob-gyns would go out of business without abortion. But, as anyone who's been walking into a clinic for a Pap smear and had someone yell, "Don't kill your baby!" can attest, they do believe it. They almost have to.

How to counter this myth when you hear it: Point out that there's a lot more money to be made from the $5,000 delivery fees than the $500 abortion fees, so if ob-gyns were really just in it for the money, they'd not only oppose abortion, they'd oppose contraception. Which is to say, they'd be antichoice. When dealing with particularly slow-witted antichoicers, it might be fun to accuse them of fronting for unscrupulous ob-gyns who want to ban abortion so they can make more money.

WOMEN WHO HAVE ABORTIONS, PARTICULARLY LATE-TERM ABORTIONS, ARE JUST AMORAL FEATHERHEADS WHO DIDN'T REALIZE THAT PREGNANCY CAN BE HELL ON YOUR WAISTLINE

Example from a man who calls himself "Publius" in the comments on my blog:

> *What can one do but wait approximately seven months to get around to having that abortion that she's been putting off? "I'll do it after I clear the gutters and the spring cleaning, I suppose"—but alas, Congress has stepped in to tell me what to do with my uterus! The horror! "I have a right to lallygag, dammit!" The uterus is, after all, the oracle of all human wisdom and perfect moral knowledge. It is quite a shame that no man has one.*

Known as the "prom dress" libel, it's the antichoice theory that women who have abortions are acting strictly out of the feminine weaknesses of vanity and bimbotude. In this particular antichoice myth, though, women can be saved from their own vapidity by forced motherhood. For as some communities must toss a virgin into the volcano to save themselves, a woman must have her body sacrificed to a baby against her will to save her from the morally degenerate view that she has a life and rights of her own.

Rarely will an antichoicer admit that a woman aborts for any other reason than the avoidance of her god-given destiny for motherhood. The prom dress libel hinges on the notion that women who have abortions are uniformly young and childless, and need to be forced into their proper roles in life. Women with children or who plan to have children in the future do not compute.

How to counter this myth when you hear it: Good luck with that. Pundits like to opine that the abortion debates are so contentious because it's a morally sticky issue. While this has some truth to it, the situation is not helped any by the fact that one side is dedicated to the belief that women are too stupid and shallow to breathe, and the other side is led mostly by women. When you're talking to someone who thinks women's defining features are "stupid" and "shallow," no matter what you say, he will hear a vague buzzing sound. If you're really dedicated, fetch a man and have him say it for you. Said man better be prepared to be told he's pussy-whipped, however.

DOCTORS WHO PROVIDE ABORTIONS EAT FETUSES

I just wish I were making this up, but no. Read antichoice propaganda long enough, and you'll find out that they're swapping stories about fetus-eating amongst each other. The right-wing website WorldNetDaily recorded one such rumor in June 2005:

> *A Kansas City abortionist is out of business after investigators discovered a grisly house of horrors at his clinic—with fetuses kept in Styrofoam cups in his refrigerator and one employee accusing him of microwaving one and stirring it into his lunch.*

The breathless accusations of fetus-eating don't stay in Kansas, either, but are flung around rather willy-nilly, though foreign providers fall under suspicion more often, no doubt because it's a lot harder to disprove fetus-eating in China than in our own backyard.

Giving in to the temptation to psychoanalyze, I'd suggest that this myth has a hold on antichoice imaginations for two reasons. Humans have a tendency to accuse their opponents of cannibalism to dehumanize them, which is why you have so many myths about "primitive" people who supposedly engaged in the practice. More importantly, I think antichoicers latch onto fetus-eating as a myth because it confirms to them that the doctor and woman are in cahoots to emasculate the impregnator. In their viewpoint, a man goes to all the effort to ejaculate into a woman, only to have her turn over the results of his hard work to her doctor, who absorbs his essence and possibly eats his soul.

How to counter this myth when you hear it: Once someone has started accusing doctors of eating fetuses, you don't really have to counter his arguments. All you have to do is make sure that his paranoid ranting is heard by people sitting on the fence, to demonstrate to them what kind of lunatics they're throwing in with if they lean to the antichoice side.

GIVE A GIRL A CONTRACEPTIVE, AND NEXT THING YOU KNOW SHE'S THROWING ORGIES

Unfortunately for the antichoice movement, they didn't rise to power under George W. Bush until after the birth control pill had been on the market for thirty-seven years, with resounding popularity that whole time. It's a tad hard to convince the majority of people who have used contraception at some point in time that their preferred methods are harbingers of Satan himself. Instead, antichoicers used their newfound power to attack newer forms of contraception, most notably a pill called Plan B, which is a contraceptive women can take after intercourse to prevent ovulation and pregnancy.

Antichoicers used the public's ignorance about how pregnancy works to agitate against selling this drug over the counter. Most people are unaware that it takes a couple of days for sperm to make their journey to the egg, and instead figure the pregnancy starts as soon as the man involved reaches the end of his final grunt, which made it easy for antichoicers to delude people into thinking that emergency contraception was some kind of abortion.

Bush's appointees in the FDA didn't have the luxury of ignorance on how pregnancy works, though, so they had to be honest that their intentions were to deprive young women of effective contraception on the theory that women who had it would go crazy and start fucking every man in sight. FDA medical officer Dr. Curtis Rosebraugh reported Bush appointee to deputy operations commissioner Dr. Janet Woodcock registering her disapproval of emergency contraception. She stated that it would create "extreme promiscuous behaviors such as the medication taking on an 'urban legend' status that would lead adolescents to form sex-based cults centered around the use of Plan B."

How to counter this myth when you hear it: Some people might wonder what the downside to sex cults for teenagers might be, particularly if some people didn't even get any on prom night when some people were teenagers. Despite this, it might not be best to bring this up. We as a nation cannot yet admit outright that people younger than twenty-one have sex—that most of us had sex prior to that age—and it's turned out okay.

Instead, attack the idea that contraception will be the end of civilization as we know it. This shouldn't be hard to do, since the vast majority of people engage in contraception use at some point and civilization hasn't collapsed. Point this out. Personalize it; say, "I've used contraception for fifteen years, and so far, I have not joined any teenage sex cults." If you're married, point out that you managed to have sex prior to marriage and use contraception without rendering yourself unmarriageable. These revelations will either throw your opponent for a loop or cause him to back away from you, lest your sinfulness is catching.

ABORTION WILL MAKE YOU SUICIDAL

In the antichoice mythology, doctors are money-grubbing seducers and women who get abortions are far too dumb to understand what they are doing when they get abortions. The logical conclusion is that many women who get abortions must, at some point down the road, wake up one day in a cold sweat and realize, "My god, I had an abortion! That must mean that I'm never going to have that particular baby. Why didn't anyone tell me?"

At this point, the woman with her newfound awareness will become profoundly depressed at not having had that baby. In the antichoice view, women are semidumb animals with an instinct to breed and will become depressed if that instinct is frustrated, just as your dog will get in a funk if you don't let him run around and pee on things.

It's unclear at times whether antichoicers are aware that women who have abortions may have had babies in the past or will have them in the future. The "suicidal" myth holds together better if you assume outright that a woman who aborts a pregnancy has blown her one shot at motherhood. Antichoicers do talk about the miracle of life with sentimental tones that imply that it is in fact a miracle, instead of a biological occurrence so common that people have to take measures to stop it, so there is the remote possibility that some of them do not fathom that many women are able to prevent and abort pregnancies while still having other opportunities to carry them out.

An entire industry has sprung up around trying to prove this theory that women become suicidal after realizing that abortion ends pregnancy. The main method of proving it is to find lonely women who've had abortions in the past, befriend them, lure them into evangelical churches, and then guilt-trip them until they "repent" their abortions and blame all their problems ever in life on the abortion, as if not having had it would make friends, a good job, or a loving husband magically appear. At this point, you can parade them around to talk about how sorry they are about the abortion, secure that few such women will rebel and lose their status in their communities.

How to counter this myth when you hear it: It's probably not enough to point out that both the American Psychiatric Association and the American Psychological Association reject the idea that there's such thing as "postabortion syndrome." If you're a masochist, you could try that and then, for dessert, find yourself a creationist to argue with about biology.

In addition to pointing out that there's no such thing as "postabortion syndrome," it's helpful to note that there is such a thing as postpartum depression. Make your antichoicer deny it. Take a swipe right at the central myth that childbirth is a universally great experience for women that takes fallen sluts and magically transforms them through labor pains into beatific mothers, as content to cradle a baby and nothing more as a dog is to chase the ball over and over again. Extra bonus points if you can get the antichoicer to drop the sentimental facade to reveal the misogynist underneath by provoking him to deride women who suffer postpartum depression.

ABORTION CAUSES BREAST CANCER

No matter how many times another study comes out disproving this, antichoicers continue to stick to their guns on this one, even trying to legislate the lie into truth with laws mandating that doctors inform abortion patients of this nonexistent risk. (So far, I've not seen any legislation that forbids the doctor from rolling her eyes while reading the mandated warning, though.) They believe it in the face of all evidence to the contrary because it seems like it should be true that Jesus punishes you for using your southern lady bits in nonapproved ways by lopping off your northern lady bits.

How to counter this myth when you hear it: As usual, invoking evidence and being reasonable won't work. Instead of relying solely on evidence, tell a little story about having a friend who is a Gold Star Lesbian—has never even seen a man naked, much less been pregnant—and she got breast cancer anyway.

What makes this strategy fun is that your opponent has probably been lulled into thinking that lesbianism and having abortions go together like peanut butter and jelly. Your comment may very well make him realize that his worldview has giant holes in it. If you see him get the blank look on his face as he tries to puzzle it out—a lesbian? Who didn't get an abortion? Because she couldn't get pregnant without sperm?—feel free to wander off and do something else, because he might be there a while trying to figure out how he never figured it out in the first place.

THE MODERATE MYTH: ABORTION IS OKAY IF DONE FOR THE "RIGHT" REASONS, BUT WRONG IF USED AS BIRTH CONTROL

The woeful American tendency to assume that the proper method for deducing the correct political stance is to take the two assigned sides in a debate and split it in the middle has led to this unfortunate myth of what the proper moderate stance on abortion should be. How to avoid using abortion as anything but a method to control your births is not spelled out. Perhaps the proper way to use abortion is to have your uterus scraped occasionally when you're not pregnant to increase your moral fortitude.

In truth, what this myth means is that the abortion moderate buys into the notion perpetuated by antichoicers that women who get abortions are dirty, stupid sluts who can't take the time out of fucking and sucking everything in sight to swallow a pill, and as such, find themselves routinely having to abort pregnancies lest the subsequent babies get in the way of future orgies. However, the moderate does want to reserve her own right or the rights of her friends, family, and lovers to obtain abortions, since they are clearly not sluts and deserve not to be burdened by unwanted pregnancy.

How to counter this myth when you hear it: The Socratic method was made to pester moderates who hold incoherent political-compromise positions. Ask the moderate how exactly she would enact the "no abortions for stupid sluts" provision in such a way that nonstupid sluts wouldn't get caught up in it. Most of the time, moderates who spout this myth haven't stopped to consider that the debate isn't whether Suzy the Town Slut is a bad person, but whether or not Suzy the Town Slut deserves her human rights. Or that someone might consider the moderate the town slut herself, or that the moderate might be a man who knocked up the town slut.

Suggested Socratic questions: Do you think that women getting abortions should sign an oath swearing they try to limit their sex partners and use contraception responsibly? Should we enact a three-abortion limit? If we do, what about the one woman who just has really bad luck with condoms and her husband? Do you think someone should sign an affidavit swearing that she knows that abortion ends a pregnancy and is not a contraceptive? Do you think anyone getting one doesn't know that?

Do Your Clothes Pass Modest Muster?

The growth spurt in Christian fundamentalism, which is no small part a reaction to the impending equality for women in America, comes, to no one's great surprise, with an accompanying obsession with snuffing out any hint of liveliness or pleasure that may crop up unbidden among its followers, particularly the young ones. A large part of this is a growing obsession with enforcing "modesty" on the women. "Modesty" is a set of hazy, hard-to-follow rules where the implied punishment for violating them is being sexually abused or shunned as a harlot. The increasing interest in defining and enforcing "modesty" among women has two major obstacles:

1. Women aren't very interested in it.

2. Trying to distinguish the Christian version of "modesty" from the one that dominates in fundamentalist Muslim communities is a challenge. A big deal has been made about how the obsession with women's dress makes these cultures somehow inferior to ours, so it wouldn't do to suddenly start imitating them outright. The trick is to imitate them while trying to somehow make it different.

Scores of catalogs, websites, and newsletters offer suggestions on what to wear in order to pass modest muster, creating a veritable uniform to signal how modest and Christian and totally not Muslim the wearer is. Apparently, the proper Christian woman can either dress like an extra on *Little House on the Prairie* or, at best, wear a lot of cheap denim dresses, as long as they have the proper bagginess and are decorated with fake flowers that would leave an early-'90s sitcom star gasping at the gaudiness.

Unsurprisingly, the ugliness of it all hasn't managed to impress the would-be Christian rock fan set. Somehow, it's critical in the twenty-first century to strike that right balance of watered-down pop culture and watered-down religious fanaticism before you can really draw the crowds. In lieu of having a Christian woman's uniform, then, there are growing attempts to lay down a set of hazy rules about what is and isn't "modest," with the implication that girls and women can have their Christian modesty while still shopping at the local mall.

One website, The Rebelution, which is run by two teenage fundamentalists of the extreme Christian rock variety, attempted to establish guidelines of modest dress somewhere between mall ho and burqa. They ran a series of questions on their website and had their male readers answer on topics varying from whether or not girls should be permitted to wear dangly earrings to whether or not messenger bags were sinful with their ability to separate, if not exactly lift, the breasts. As can be imagined, given the chance to boss young women around on what to wear, many young men stepped up to the plate and indicated, firmly, that women pretty much can't win. But that comes as no surprise to the feminist reader.

Unfortunately, they have a long way to go to convey the message that one can somehow find a "modest" form of dress that is hip enough not to make one feel like one is dressed to go churn some butter. While there were plenty of questions involving lengths of hemlines and whether or not having "WWJD" across your chest makes young men think too much of boobs, there were plenty of other questions that went unasked, questions that might make the entire operation seem hipper.

- How many visible tattoos before one is immodest? Two, three, twelve? Can someone have so many visible tattoos that she becomes sexually unappealing to her brothers in Christ, making her tattooed into de facto modesty? Do weeping martyr tattoos count as pro-modesty points while naked lady tattoos count against you in the modesty department?
- If you wear a band T-shirt, can you be more or less modest depending on the band? For instance, does a "secular" rock band rate as more immodest than a Christian rock band? Do you become more modest the more the band on your T-shirt sucks?
- Does being pregnant count against you in the modesty department? After all, you are displaying rather definitive evidence that you Do It. Does it help you regain your modesty if you wear infantilizing maternity clothes, preferably with bows and duckies?
- On that note, can you become a born-again virgin while still pregnant?
- Are tongue piercings more immodest than nose piercings? How about clit piercings? Are they the most modest because they are the easiest to hide under your clothes?
- Are pointy-toed high heels more modest than round-toe high heels? Pointy-toed shoes are more punishing and crippling, which would incline one to think they are more modest. However, they don't have the wholesome goodness that round-toe shoes have. Minnie Mouse wears round-toe high heels, but Carrie Bradshaw wears pointy-toed shoes.

- If you wear a head scarf to indicate that you're of the super-modest variety, does it detract from the effect if the scarf is leopard-print? Can you be a modest harlot?
- If you wear a sorority sweatshirt, is it more immodest if the house has a reputation on campus for housing loose women, even if the reputation isn't deserved?
- Is there something deeply immodest about cutting all the twee little bows that manufacturers put on women's underwear? Right there on the front of many a bra or pair of panties, it will lie, the crappy little bow. Snipping it off seems an act of feminist rebellion, somehow, declaring that this piece of underwear is not for little girls but for grown women. That seems like it's probably immodest.
- Open-toed shoes are almost certainly more immodest than close-toed shoes, but what if you have really ugly feet? Do crusty, ill-kempt feet in cute sandals rate as more modest than feet hidden in close-toed shoes?
- On that note, does the modesty of a low-cut shirt depend on how much boob you have to fill it out? If you're an A-cup, no matter how low the neckline plunges, you're probably not going to see much curve unless it actually scoops under the breast. If so, is that really fair to our bustier sisters?
- Are Birkenstocks the most modest shoe of all?

So many questions, and yet the biggest one of all is how this can even be a big-time discussion in the twenty-first century in America. One of the young men at The Rebelution laid out what was at stake in spelling out the modesty rules for young women when he said, "The female body is a powerful gift, intended for one man." Reading that, it appears the most modest dress of all is a giant gift-wrapped box that you don't remove until your selected husband pulls off the bow. Sure, you'll start to smell a bit ripe after a while, but at least the message is unmistakable.

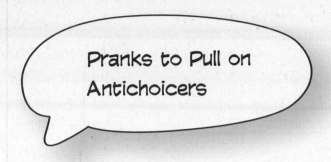

Pranks to Pull on Antichoicers

Because reproductive-rights politics are so dreary and serious all the time.

PRANK-CALL CRISIS PREGNANCY CENTERS

In the days prior to *Roe v. Wade,* white, middle-class families who had pregnant but unwed girls on their hands often squirreled them away in maternity homes, where they would be hidden from the world to give birth and then have their baby put up for adoption so they could rejoin the world and pretend it never happened. Those places largely disappeared after abortion was legalized, but the snatch-the-baby spirit behind them lives on in crisis pregnancy centers. CPCs are places that try to lure pregnant women with promises of some kind of medical care or psychological counseling. Once women are there, the CPCs spend all their effort in trying to discourage an abortion. Sometimes they will encourage the woman to relinquish the baby to adoption services. Often, they disguise themselves as a women's clinic, or set up near a real women's clinic in the hopes that they can snag some of the clinic's patients. They are evil.

However, they are good for a laugh if you enjoy prank calls. In college, my friends and I would prank-call these places and set up appointments, making our stories increasingly maudlin. There seemed to be no limit on who they thought constituted a suitable mother for a salvageable, adoptable baby. Twelve years old? Have it. Smoking PCP on a daily basis? Have it. Your father would kill you? You should definitely have it. Even more fun is to ask about the services they offer, to hear them squirm. Pregnancy testing? You mean, the kind you can buy for $10 at the grocery store? Ten dollars doesn't seem like too steep a price to pay to avoid having to sit through a video berating you about how your basic rights are an offense to Jesus.

Word of warning on all prank calls: If you have a speaker phone, make sure that everyone in the room is equipped with a throw pillow to stifle their laughter.

PROTEST ANTICHOICE ORGANIZATIONS

Give back to them what they have given so richly to women. Gather up some compadres, make some signs, and hit the parking lots. Coming up with signs will be half the fun, especially since there are endless variations on telling people to go fuck themselves. Other suggestions: MAKE MORE LIBERALS—BAN ABORTION; NOT EVERYONE WANTS TO ADVERTISE HOW MUCH SEX THEY'RE HAVING BY HEAD COUNTS; and a perennial favorite on the blogs, THE VAGINA IS NOT A CLOWN CAR.

PREGNANT NUN PROTESTS

You and your friends, dressed as pregnant nuns, shoving your way to the front of an antichoice protest. What your signs say is up to you, because the sight of you will be sufficient to create enough confusion that a few patients might be able to sneak through to the clinic without being harassed.

SIGN 'EM UP

Get dressed in a suit or some other business wear and show up at an abortion clinic protest with a clipboard. Explain to people that you're from the Children's Bureau and you're here to sign all the volunteers up to adopt babies. Make it very clear that since there's already a waiting list for healthy white infants, they're going on the other adoption waiting list, for babies who aren't so easily snatched up by adoptive parents. Be chirpy about it: "The good news is that you won't have to wait for your new baby like the people on the other waiting list!" If people decline to sign up, act genuinely confused. "But the Bureau told me you were here to convince women not to have abortions. What other reason would you have for getting into someone else's private business, if not because you want the babies?" If they continue to decline, pull out another clipboard and start filling out a receipt. "Well, we do have a backup plan for the care and feeding of the babies you insist should be born but don't want to raise yourself. How much should I put you down for? Before college tuition, raising one child for eighteen years will probably come in at $250,000. We'll also need to pay the mother for her time and pay the state for handling the baby, so tack on another $50,000. Will that be check or charge?"

VIDEOTAPE THE STAMMERING

Actually, you don't need to do this, because a group of pranksters in Libertyville, Illinois, went to an antichoice demonstration with a video camera and started asking protesters the simple question, "If abortion is made illegal, what should happen to women who get abortions?" One protester after another stammered, looked like the questioner had just asked them to give the definitive meaning of life, or acted like they'd been offered Sophie's Choice. One thing was certain—none of them had thought their political stance on choice through at all. Few things are more humiliating than finding out that you've spent a weekend or two a month protesting and carrying on about an issue you haven't really thought over in any logical way at all.

But just because someone has pulled this prank once doesn't mean that it can't be done again. Imagine what would happen if antichoicers genuinely feared that they couldn't go to protests without the danger of having someone ask them to think about policy instead of weeping and carrying on about the great tragedy that women are fucking and getting away with it.

DEMONSTRATE ON BEHALF OF THE MINISTRY OF TRUTH

Get a group of female friends together and have overalls printed up that say MINISTRY OF TRUTH on them. Pair the overalls off with colorful JUNIOR ANTISEX LEAGUE sashes, and you're ready to join a clinic protest. Don't worry about anyone catching the *1984* reference—at least among the protesters. The words "ministry" and "truth" will lull them into believing you're just one of the four million antichoice groups hating women for Jesus. Play it completely straight, talking only in *1984*-speak about the dangers of sex and the way that it provokes the imagination. Hopefully, you'll give some clinic workers or defenders a chuckle. Take lots of pictures and send them to me.

Part 5.

YOU DON'T NEED GOD TO TELL YOU TO BE SEXIST

Myths About Feminists

Being a modern feminist is hard enough even when dealing with people who know what feminism is all about. To add to your problems, however, there are many myths out there about feminists, to the point that it's useful to think of antifeminist attacks as being made upon a straw feminist, a useful tool for backlash article writers and other sundry antifeminists. Real feminists don't make real good targets, seeing as how we refuse to behave and fit into the stereotypes appointed to us so people can hate us in lieu of actually coming out against women's equality.

No doubt you're aware of most of the common myths about feminists, but it's always fun to review them in one place.

FEMINISTS THINK THERE'S NO DIFFERENCE BETWEEN MEN AND WOMEN

Very much untrue. Feminists in fact are desperately trying to get Congress, the Supreme Court, and the nation at large to understand that no matter how much some men sincerely believe otherwise, uteruses only exist in female bodies and therefore women should be the decision-makers when it comes to how said uteruses are used.

FEMINISTS HATE MEN

This myth is frequently trotted out by the exact same people who think that we think we are men. That said, there is a little-known fact that male dominance and the biological reality of men are one and the same thing, due to a curse laid on half the human race by the wicked Witch Mispenasa. It's said that if ever women should achieve equality with men, men will cease to exist altogether. So if feminists are fighting against male dominance, we have no choice but to believe they are out to destroy men themselves.

FEMINISTS ARE JUST TOO UGLY TO GET A MAN

Which is what we want, because we hate men so much. Strangely, the act of trotting out the smoking hot Gloria Steinem repeatedly and pointing at her and saying, "See?" hasn't done a damn thing to curtail this myth. It's almost as if people want to believe it so badly they are ignoring the evidence against it.

FEMINISTS HATE CHILDREN

Only people who have lost touch with reality altogether could think that it's child-hating to demand a world where every child born is a wanted child, and where society cares what happens to children after they are born.

FEMINISTS HATE SEX

Not true, but what is true is that it's physically painful to refrain from saying, "With you, sure," to any man who says this. But refrain we do, because god forbid we be accused of lowering the tone of the discourse.

FEMINISTS ARE JUST SLUTS WHO WANT AN EXCUSE TO HAVE SEX ALL THE TIME

This is concurrent with the belief that feminists are all sex-hating prudes. Often, the same person holds both beliefs at once, a phenomenon that really could stand more research. This one is also not true, except for that one wild weekend when we all got together and there was too much vodka consumed. Yes, feminists do have annual meetings where everyone gets together, but that's not technically a myth so much as a secret.

FEMINISTS ARE A BUNCH OF ABORTION-LOVING DYKES

Best example of this stereotype, culled from a comment by a user of the right-wing forum Free Republic: "I thank Mary [Cheney] for having the baby and not having an abortion. Kudos for her on that anyway." Mary Cheney, the daughter of Vice President Dick Cheney, is in fact a lesbian. However, there is no reason to think she is a feminist or that she gets artificially inseminated for the thrill of having abortions on a regular basis.

FEMINISTS ARE UPPER-MIDDLE-CLASS WHITE WOMEN WHO ARE JUST BORED AND HAVE NOTHING BETTER TO DO

While for personal reasons, I do indeed wish this was true, I have to admit that when someone asked me if I was making the max contribution to my IRA every year, my answer was, "What's that?" Make of that what you will.

FEMINISTS HAVE NO SENSE OF HUMOR

This particular myth is something of a red herring. Men who trot this out generally think that women have no sense of humor, at least if you define "sense of humor" as "ability to generate humorous comments." Where feminists get accused of having no sense of humor is that we fail in our mandatory female mission to giggle helplessly at jokes about how much we suck for being born female. Within that narrow definition of "sense of humor," it's easy to see that feminists probably don't have one.

FEMINISTS THINK THERE'S SOMETHING SO BAD ABOUT RAPE

This one would actually be true. We're no fun like that.

FEMINISTS DON'T SHAVE

Technically true, but mostly because we are so well-versed in the practice of witchcraft. Call it shallow to make your first spell the one that forces your body hair to quit growing, but trust me, you'll enjoy having that extra fifteen to twenty minutes a day you used to spend shaving.

FEMINISTS THINK EMASCULATING PICTURES OF HALF-NAKED MEN IN POLKA-DOT PANTIES ARE FUNNY

Depends on the context. Some say this is slightly less funny if the man in the picture is your husband and the pictures are something of a surprise.

The Funny/Unfunny Double Bind

eminists are humorless, right? That's what we're always hearing, that feminists go around with dour faces when talking about boring subjects like why rape needs to stop or why abortion should be legal, a tedious topic that implies that what happens to a woman after she's been fucked matters one whit to anyone. Get a sense of humor! Quit looking so sad, or worse angry, just because people are putting you down and pissing you off.

Sometimes, with all these stereotypes of humorless feminists flying around, a gal starts to get the impression that if you just show that feminist-minded women are often rather funny, then people will learn and move on. And that's where such a gal is wrong. Feminists are supposed to be humorless, and woe unto one who bucks that expectation. Next thing you know, some right-winger is on TV, bemoaning how the mean ladies made him feel small with their jokes and their funny business. (Though this isn't necessarily bad, because when it happened to me, I had the pleasure of another right-winger agreeing with the first one that the funny lady made him sad, bobbing his head up and down over his bizarre little bowtie in angry agreement that women who make jokes suck. Having Tucker Carlson hate you is good for a round of beers when you admit it at some of your finer alcohol-dispensing establishments.)

Be unfunny and no one takes you seriously. Be funny and massive social disapproval awaits you. Variations of the outrage you can expect:

HUMOR FROM WOMEN MAKES BABY JESUS CRY

This irritating complaint from the misogynists of the world will often propel itself to national headlines, making it exponentially more irritating. The best-known case is when Roseanne Barr, not known for her delicate feminine unwillingness to engage in genuinely funny jokes, made national headlines when she was invited to sing the national anthem at a baseball game. She did what she was hired to do, which was have some fun with it, by singing it in a grating voice and grabbing her crotch and spitting, in what's commonly known as a "joke." However, legions of Americans, true believers that you can't tell a joke and maintain a uterus at the same time, sprung into offended mode. Roseanne was insufficiently pious toward baseball, national anthems about war, and the male-only right to grab your crotch! She might as well have castrated Joe DiMaggio on national television. Women are supposed to treat all things patriarchal—which means pretty much everything—with total reverence at all times, and anything short of that is enough to send the sum of Conservative Nation into a faint, which they will only be roused from by the sound of Bill O'Reilly angrily condemning something. The problem with this is it precludes you from making jokes most of the time, because impiety is a central component to really good humor. Not that this restriction bothers Conservative Nation much, since you probably should be scrubbing or sucking something instead of cracking jokes anyway.

IF YOU'RE FUNNY, CHRISTOPHER HITCHENS DOESN'T WANT TO FUCK YOU

In an article in the January 2007 edition of *Vanity Fair* where he wondered why women weren't very funny, he got all tangled up when he remembered that many women are indeed funny. But he decided that didn't threaten him (even though it should, since he's not very funny), because he finds them pleasingly unfuckable. "In any case, my argument doesn't say that there are no decent women comedians. There are more terrible female comedians than there are terrible male comedians, but there are some impressive ladies out there. Most of them, though, when you come to review the situation, are hefty or dykey or Jewish, or some combo of the three."

Having a litany of people that Hitchens won't fuck—funny women, hefty women, dykey women, or Jewish women—rattled off to you is sort of like listening to a governor read off a list of pardons. All you can do is think about their good fortune and wish them well. But the general lesson remains, which is that women who are funny can expect to be told not only that they give some men the vapors, but also that they render themselves unable to inspire erections in such vapored men.

MAKE A JOKE AND HAVE EVERYONE SIMPLY PRETEND THAT DIDN'T HAPPEN

There was a troubling period of my life where I was dating a guy who stole my jokes. Worse, even, I would tell a joke and everyone would laugh and then later, they would remember it as if he told the joke. It was uncanny and weird and discouraging, but a good sign of the way that female humor, and feminist humor in particular, is almost unconsciously thrown down the memory hole.

That said, after we broke up, I had to wonder if his friends were alarmed at the precipitous decline in the number of jokes he was telling.

YOU'LL BE INVITED TO SIT ON THE PSYCHOANALYST'S COUCH

One of the strangest, but by no means uncommon, reactions a feminist cracking jokes can get is to be put on the couch by people who assume that women's default status is crazy. It's strange, because putting someone on the couch for cracking jokes assumes wrongly that there's a reason, besides wanting to be funny, to try to be funny. Hillary Clinton found this out the hard way in 2007, when, responding to a question about her confidence in fighting terrorism, she made a crack about how she had experience handling evil men. Yes, the joke wasn't especially funny, but bombing is usually not a reason to treat someone like they're two steps from the loony bin. But in her case, a multitude of articles and TV shows analyzed the joke to death. Why did she tell the joke? Was she trying to hurt her husband? Mock the media? Equate adultery with terrorism?

That she might be trying to get a laugh was not analyzed, naturally. Why would a woman want to make people laugh when she knows that could cause undue alarm?

> ## Feminism Versus Chivalry, or I Opened a Door for You so Now I Can Be a Douchebag

Feminists should realize that our enemies have basically given up when they resort to citing chivalry as an argument against women's equality. "Feminism will bring an end to chivalry" isn't really so much of an argument as an impotent threat. The nonargument, rephrased for clarity, is, "Nice pedestal you got there. Be a shame if something happened to it."

The various things that we're told women are in dire threat of losing if we actually achieve equality with men compose a list that is truly distressing. In fact, it might not be too much to say that many women would perish without these important benefits we accrue in exchange for inequality.

MEN WILL QUIT OPENING DOORS FOR YOU

Having never opened a door for myself, the mere thought of it does send a chill down the spine. Are these doors heavy? Will my spindly arms strain or break under the stress of trying to pry one of these doors open? If I die from the effort of trying to push open my front door, will my cats feast on my never-married corpse before anyone discovers I'm dead?

MEN WILL QUIT BUYING DINNER OR DRINKS FOR YOU

Luckily, once women are making the 25 percent more on average they'll have to make in order to be equal with men, the blow from this financially devastating loss of up to a couple dozen dollars a month will be softened some.

MEN WILL QUIT PULLING OUT CHAIRS FOR YOU OR HELPING YOU WITH YOUR COAT

Our foremothers should have thought about how bad it would suck to eat all our meals sitting on the floor and spend all our winter months shivering coatless before they marched for the right to vote. Voting is fun and all, but not when you're fighting the dog for your side of mashed potatoes.

MARRIAGE WILL BECOME IMPOSSIBLE WHEN MEN GO ON A PROPOSAL STRIKE

Yes, I've actually heard this argument. Needless to say, the young man making it wasn't about to listen to the brilliant solution where mixed-gender marriage is banned and same-sex marriage is perfectly legal, making this entire conundrum irrelevant.

MEN WILL MAKE YOU WALK HOME ALL ALONE, LEAVING YOU TO THE RAPISTS

Never mind that statistically speaking, you're likelier to get raped by the guy who walked you home than by the guy lurking in the bushes. Truth told, when was the last time some guy walked you home simply out of the goodness of his heart, and not because he was hoping if he hung around long enough, you might find yourself called upon to fuck him? Or for that matter, are cabs really that impossible to find in pedestrian-friendly cities?

MEN WILL QUIT BRINGING HOME THE BACON

Nine times out of ten, the man making this threat means more that he hopes that if he hates on feminism hard enough, the courts will suddenly decree that he doesn't have to pay child support anymore. As you can imagine, the infrequency of this magical event leaves in its wake a series of extremely bitter men, the sort who run around threatening to quit walking home the women they weren't walking home anyway.

A Humor Primer for Those Who Don't Hate Women

In 2007, there was a controversy at University of Western Ontario when the student newspaper, in an attempt to lampoon campus feminists, resorted to the old trick of mixing up fantasies of raping the opinions out of uppity bitches with humor, writing what was supposed to be a funny parody of the Take Back the Night rallies. To be fair, mixing up rape fantasies with jokes is a common mistake made by young men whose brains have backed up from what you might call the sexual frustration induced by a mixture of wanting sex with women and anger that women come fully equipped with vocal cords and brains, a feature that *Maxim* magazine forgot to warn them about.

Still, in the spirit of progressive feminist inclusiveness, I thought it might be time to reach out to the jerkoffs who write articles like the one in the University of Western Ontario *Gazette* by explaining what makes the jokes so damn funny to this mostly feminist audience. See, most of us tend to fall in the spectrum of "normal" people who expect that humor is funny because it references things that are true, and just shake our heads in frustration at people who make jokes that use the fantasy world shown in porn as a frame of reference. We should be sympathetic. These young men are victims, too, after all, even though they don't realize how badly they've crippled themselves by sitting inside all day jerking off to porn in lieu of interacting with actual human beings. No wonder they're angry when they meet women in the real world who don't behave like porn has taught them women do.

The article's humor got off to an unreal start with the title, "Labia Majora Carnage." To ordinary people, this title seems to be structured like a pun of some sort, but if you peel back the layers, there is nothing there. It would be like pushing open the labia majora to find a blank slate, no vagina, no clitoris, nothing. But in the porn-addled brain, this joke is hilarious, because any reference to the fact that women don't have the organs to jerk off with is funny. What do they do with their time? It's a mystery, but a funny mystery.

Further quotes give us more insight into what constitutes "humor" for those who have mental breakdowns from nonstop computer-enhanced masturbation.

The march was led by members of Western's Women's Issues Network, who, for the first time all year, left their circle in the University Community Centre, where witnesses claim they perform tribal dances and yell alienating slurs about pussies and cunts.

In order to understand this joke, you must accept a couple of basic premises:

1. It's wrong for women to have fun, period, but it's much worse if they experience pleasure without involving men. Thus, women dancing among themselves is funny like a dog in a clown costume walking on two legs is funny to a five-year-old. It's so out of place!

2. Women mentioning that they have cunts is "alienating." After all, to the porn-addled young man, a woman in jeans who claims she has a cunt must be lying her fool head off. Since real women doff their clothes and fuck you the second the soundtrack in your mind starts, and these women aren't doing that, it's probably because they're hiding the fact that they're freakishly smooth down there, like Barbie dolls. Talking about your vagina without immediately proffering it to all comers for fucking is false advertisement, in other words.

The next step to being humorous through this sexist lens is to joke about *The Vagina Monologues* without bothering to see the play and learn enough about what you're mocking to mock it properly.

> *"My vagina told me she hates thongs . . . they're far too restrictive," said Jennifer Ostrich, a vocal WIN member. "And what my vagina wants, my vagina gets. Nighties are far more comfortable and practical. They let my vagina be free to the world so she can speak out and say whatever she wants."*

This is funny because it's assumed that women think of themselves as nothing more than vaginas, because porn-addled young men think of women as nothing but vaginas and assume that's a universal assumption. *The Vagina Monologues* can safely be assumed to be a place where women communicate the fact that their vaginas, so silent on the computer monitor, *actually speak up when men and/or cameras are not around,* which means, naturally, that men should never allow a vagina to walk around unmonitored.

> *Near the end of the march, chaos broke out when Ostrich's vagina crawled from under [her] flowing white nightie, stole a loudspeaker and went on a rampage.*

This is funny because vaginas are scary. Get too close to one, it'll go on a rampage and bite your dick off. Better to leave the vaginas on the screen, where they can't leap out and hurt you.

"You don't know me, bee-otch," [the vagina] squealed. "You can't even see me through all this hair you've let over-grow. Think of me. I can't even breathe down here!"

Just as men whose brains have been addled by antichoice propaganda assume that the silent fetuses actually speak for them, so does the porn-addled author assume that silent vaginas somehow have opinions that tailor exactly to his desires. In sum, all those women who don't use their vaginas exactly as he would like them to are overruling their vagina-masters' wishes and are completely out of line.

Upon seeing the chaos, London Police Chief Murray Faulkner stopped greasing his nightstick and intervened.

He grabbed the loudspeaker from Ostrich's wild vagina and took it into a dark alley to teach it a lesson.

To Ostrich's dismay, the vagina followed, giggling as it said, "I love it when a man in uniform takes control."

The belief that women really want to be raped is one of the biggest breaks with reality made by the misogynist mind. You don't really even have to generate reality-based statistics and figures to demonstrate that women don't want to be raped. It's a tautological issue—since rape is defined as being forced to have sex against your will, if you want to have sex, you are hardly being raped.

What might be interesting is seeing how much absorbing the idea that "no means yes" can condition an addled young man into becoming a flaming wingnut. After all, once you practice believing that "no means yes," you're primed to start believing that war is peace and ignorance is strength.

Women were delighted to see groups of men standing on the sidewalks in support.

"It was so great to see men supporting us in our nighties and helping us to spread vagina peace and love," [one woman] said.

One man held a sign that read, "Yeah baby, I'll take back your nightie anytime!"

To those of us in the real world, a joke about how women don't know they're being sexually harassed makes no sense, because we realize that women are acutely aware of all the abuse they take simply for being women. However, in the misogynist's fantasy world, women are extraordinarily stupid. The tradition of porn-addled men trying to convince themselves that women are stupid has a long history to it. *Playboy* magazine really broke out in this area, by running a long series of comics called *Little Annie Fanny,* which—while being much funnier than anything a bunch of frat boys yukking it up at a school newspaper could come up with—was still based around the premise that women neither are aware of the effect that their heaving bosoms have on men, nor do we realize that men are having a grand old time mocking us for being women. Both assumptions are more porn-based than reality-based.

With the belief that women are too stupid to know sexual harassment when it happens to them, one has to wonder whether men who holler at women from cars are under the impression that the women are too stupid to assess the situation properly. If so, when women pointedly ignore such sidewalk abuse, do these guys realize they're being ignored? Or do they simply think they've pulled one over on their victim? All the more reason to carry pepper spray with us, so that our displeasure with being harassed cannot be mistaken for anything else.

> For the Sake of Honesty, We Must Discuss Your Lack of Fuckability at Length and in Great Detail

O f all sexist weirdo stances out there, my favorite might be the one held by guys who have made it their grim duty in life to make sure that they share the important news with women everywhere that we are insufficient sex objects and no man "really" could find us hot. No need to thank these guys, ladies. They really do wish they didn't have to tell you about your objective unsexiness, but they simply must for the sake of honesty.

My favorite example of this genre is John Derbyshire's melancholic but oh-so-honest musings in the *National Review Online* in late 2005, when he explained that women become undesirable sometime between the prom and high school graduation.

Did I buy, or browse, a copy of the November 17 GQ, in order to get a look at Jennifer Aniston's bristols? No, I didn't. While I have no doubt that Ms. Aniston is a paragon of charm, wit, and intelligence, she is also 36 years old. Even with the strenuous body-hardening exercise routines now compulsory for movie stars, at age 36 the forces of nature have won out over the view-worthiness of the unsupported female bust.

It is, in fact, a sad truth about human life that beyond our salad days,
very few of us are interesting to look at in the buff. Added to that sadness is
the very unfair truth that a woman's salad days are shorter than a man's—
really, in this precise context, only from about 15 to 20.

An outcry from women everywhere made him turn some months later to writing a long tribute to Nabokov's novel *Lolita* for evidence for his opinion that women become unfuckable as soon as they become legally fuckable. *National Review* watchers everywhere enjoyed that defense thoroughly and continue to hope for a follow-up about how he learned about the great windmill menace from *Don Quixote.*

While Derbyshire may have set the standard in the art of making sweeping generalizations about the ease in which a woman slides from beautiful to wretched, sexists everywhere enjoy the sport of arguing that the basic skill of being an erection-generating sex object is right out of the hands of the vast majority of women. Why? It's a simple way to put women into a situation where they have no good defenses. If you immediately start to argue that a diversity of women can so be attractive, then you have permitted the implicit argument—that women should strive to be worthy sex objects for the sleazy kind of guys who make these kind of statements—stand unchallenged.

In October 2006, Charles Mudede at the blog for the *Stranger,* Seattle's alt-weekly newspaper, thought he'd have some fun pushing this particular button and letting women know they simply cannot win. In this case, he argued that pregnancy made women deeply unattractive and that pregnant women should give up having sex because there's no way that they could be humping anything but what you might call a pity erection:

Sex with a pregnant women is not right or wrong but dishonest. It's an act
that is close to pity. One does it because one is trying to be nice, and not
being honest about how much [one's] partner's body has changed.

> *The body that had the sex that resulted in the pregnancy is not the*
> *same as the body that is in the process of producing a whole new life. The*
> *first body was attractive (like a flower is attractive); the pregnant body,*
> *on the other hand, is used up by the function of the pregnancy. What a*
> *woman loses in the long process of a pregnancy is precisely what made the*
> *pregnancy possible, the flower of her body.*

Mudede found out later, much to his surprise, that after pregnant women turn to fruit, they are not actually covered with wax and put out in produce bins to be sold for $1.49 a pound.

Men who try to start debates on the ease with which women become fundamentally unfuckable want one thing and one thing only—to have both women and men fall all over ourselves trying to get them to change their minds, which makes them feel like their opinion matters. Also, by arguing with them, you accidentally buy into the premise that a woman's worth can be determined by whether some crabby loser claims to find her fleetingly attractive. Sometimes it's the idea that no woman over a certain very young age could be attractive, and sometimes the argument is a variation on the one Mudede uses, which is that women become used up by sex. Regardless, the hallmark of the strategy is to make a blanket assertion that women's status as sex objects is incredibly fleeting. So if you come across some sexist trying to make himself feel important with this strategy, I advise frustrating the underlying desire.

Sample lines:

- "How nice for you. But how much nicer for the inflatable doll industry to have you as a repeat customer, since mortal women don't do it for you."
- "Agreed. I also believe that men lose their sexual attractiveness the day they have to start shaving once a day."

- "I was so relieved the day that I got too old/pregnant/unvirginal to be considered sexually attractive to creepy dudes, myself. Thanks for reminding me how good it felt to be free of annoying attention from guys like you."
- "Really now, ever since they invented Viagra, men with your problem have no reason any longer to cast the blame on the whole of womanhood. Surely your insurance can help you out with that."

Being Told to Smile by Strangers

We've all had it happen. You're sitting in public, or more likely just walking down the street, and you're lost in thoughts that leave you unlikely to be grinning manically at every stray man who passes.

"Did I leave the stove on when I left the house this morning? Why would I have the stove on when I wasn't cooking anything? How unfair is it that I'm concerned about this remote possibility? Who do I blame?"

"Goddamn motherfucking bastard. I cannot believe he thought it was a good idea to call me at four in the morning and beg for me to listen to his excuses. I guess he thought the groggier I was, the more naive I'd be."

"If Wonder Woman was from the Isle of Lesbos, doesn't that make her a Lesbian? I wonder if her boyfriend What's His Name knows this. I guess that's why we always think of her boyfriend as 'What's His Name.'"

"I am so so so happy! Life is great! Sun is shining, spring in my step! I just wish I could grin manically at every person who passes, but I know if I do that, some dweeb will come up and start hitting on me and then get mad when I tell him that just because I'm smiling doesn't mean I'm automatically going to sleep with him."

Regardless of the thought that's causing you not to be smiling at that particular moment, it's irritating when some stranger interrupts that thought so he can order you to smile. It's usually a drive-by thing, where the stranger barks the order at you and gets out of the way, having done his good deed for the day in reminding a random woman that she shouldn't forget that her first duty to the world is to provide a vacant but pleasing smile to everyone she encounters.

Because they flee the scene of the crime so quickly, it's hard to retaliate against the "Smile!" assholes. Whatever you do, don't smile, though. There's always an off chance that they'll give a follow-up glance, and they certainly don't deserve the satisfaction.

Many women have wondered what motivates the "Smile!" brigade. It's hard to say, because their tactic of attacking women who are lost in thought and then fleeing the scene makes them elusive. Many theories abound, too many to shove into this slip of a survival guide, but the many theories have broken into two camps.

THEY'RE THE SAME GUYS WHO YELL "CUNT!" AT WOMEN FROM CARS

The reason that this theory has credence is because telling a woman to smile and calling her a cunt convey the same message, which is that the man is reminding you that no matter how much you may think that you deserve to quietly think about your own things, in his eyes you're nothing but a sex object. The reason that this guy is telling you to smile instead of calling you a cunt, in this theory, is that you're both pedestrians and the latter insult might be enough to make you chase him down and tackle him. According to this theory, if he was driving by you, he'd almost surely roll down his window and interrupt your thoughts by yelling, "Cunt!"

THEY'RE NOT THE SAME GUYS WHO YELL "CUNT!" AT WOMEN FROM CARS

This camp holds that these men—while certainly out of line and conveying the message that you owe them a smile simply because you're in public and a second-class citizen—somehow simply mean well when they tell you to smile. The idea behind this theory is that such men are simply blind to their privilege and probably think that women like being told to smile. This theory is sweet, but it's hard to believe that there are a lot of men out there telling women to smile with a generous but misguided spirit. If there were such men, surely some would step forward and sheepishly admit they do this but didn't know better. To date, this hasn't happened, leading many to believe that well-meaning "Smile!" tyrants probably do not exist.

Whichever theory is true, the main thing to remember is that if you're told to smile by strange men, the problem is not you. Far too many lovely, no doubt smiley, women get told to smile and think, "Is there something wrong with me? Am I especially dour and off-putting? Do babies shriek as I walk by? Do dogs snarl and growl?" There's nothing wrong with you.

After all, what would be a lot creepier is if all women walked around all the time with vacant, robotic grins on our faces like some sort of fembot army. And even if we wanted to pull that off and could pull that off, it wouldn't do jack to stop men from yelling "Cunt!" at us from inside passing cars.

How to Decide Whether to Out Someone

Sometimes in life you just happen to discover that someone you know who is presenting as heterosexual might not be quite what he or she seems. Sometimes you happen up on evidence that said person might be gay by stumbling on that person in a public bathroom or in a dark corner doing something with a member of the same sex, and sometimes you accidentally photograph the local Baptist minister after following him into a gay bar. Either way, you have the power to out someone, so the question is whether or not to do it.

Outing is a controversial subject. Some people say it's never right, but some of us are permanent rascals and say there are plenty of good reasons to out certain people. As one of those rascals, I've cobbled together a list of when it's appropriate to come out with evidence you have that a person may be a lot more queer than they're letting on.

IS YOUR TARGET A PROFESSIONAL "EX-GAY"?

Hard as it may be to believe, the Christian right actually pays people money to go around the country telling people that they were once gay, but through the power of Jesus Christ they've given up their enthusiasm for the sex they prefer and have learned to copulate joylessly with their new spouses in the hopes that they produce enough children to calm the gossip. If your target makes a dime off pretending he or she was once gay but has left it behind, and you know otherwise, they're outable.

IS YOUR TARGET A PROPONENT OF ABSTINENCE-ONLY EDUCATION?

Abstinence-only teaches that you have to abstain until marriage. Since gays and lesbians can't get married, that means they have to abstain forever. Looking for sleazy ways to deny other people sexual satisfaction their entire lives while pursuing a little for yourself on the side is reason enough to forsake your right not to be outed.

HAS YOUR TARGET EVER USED THE PHRASE "THE HOMOSEXUAL AGENDA" WITH A STRAIGHT FACE?

If so, there's no room for him in the closet.

IS YOUR TARGET A POLITICIAN WHO HAS EVER VOTED AGAINST GAY RIGHTS?

Then out him. If he's ever highlighted a vote against gay rights in any of his campaign materials, make sure that you publish the pictures and highlight the salacious details in your press release to pay him back.

IS YOUR TARGET A RELIGIOUS LEADER FROM A CHURCH THAT PEDDLES IN HOMOPHOBIC FEAR-MONGERING?

Throw him out of the closet and follow it up with a number of public comments pitying his wife for her immense burden trying to hold together a sham marriage because she thinks it's what God wants her to do.

DOES YOUR TARGET MAKE ANY MONEY OPINING ON HOW GAYS ARE TEARING AT THE FABRIC OF AMERICAN SOCIETY?

Out him. If he works for Fox News, see if they'll take an exclusive for the outing. If they resist, threaten to go to their biggest rival in the ratings with it to see if they'll cave. The ad revenue potential from publishing photos of someone like Bill O'Reilly with a cock in his mouth would be too great for even Fox News to deny.

HAS YOUR TARGET EVER MADE HUGE FINANCIAL OR POLITICAL GAINS FROM SOMEONE ELSE'S HOMOPHOBIC FEAR-MONGERING?

This covers people like Rupert Murdoch or George W. Bush, who never get their own hands dirty but are happy to cash in on their underlings who hate-monger. Bush, for instance, generally plays dumb on the subject of gay rights, but he was happy to accept each and every vote that was dredged up by antigay activists raising the alarm about gay marriage in the 2004 election. If anyone got a picture of him in a gay bar, she would deserve the Medal of Honor for outing him.

IS YOUR TARGET MARY CHENEY?

Just kidding. When John Kerry "outed" Mary Cheney in a 2004 presidential debate, it was already well known that Mary Cheney was a lesbian. You can't out the already out, no matter what pearl-clutching pundits would have you believe.

Part 6.

POSTFEMINISM MY ASS

The Argument over Identity Politics, Summarized in a One-Act Play

Wingnuts: (singing) We love oppressing the women! Get back in the kitchen, you, and make us a baby!

Women: That's it! We're not taking any more of this!

Wingnuts: Who is this "we" you speak of?

The End

Feminists Who Are Not: Feminists for Life

In descending order of likelihood to be taken seriously as feminists by the media and by everyday people, you have first the "equity feminists," who'll I describe in the next chapter, and then you have the Feminists for Life, an antichoice group that tries to argue that repealing women's reproductive rights is somehow feminist. Feminists for Life has a little bit of esteem because it is a bona fide organization with the word "feminist" right there in the title. They also have wised up to the fact that they should offer nominal support to a handful of feminist policy proposals that could reduce the abortion rate, such as government-subsidized daycare, though their actual activism in obtaining these things is meager to absent.

HABITAT

For all the hand-wringing on their website about their concerns for the poor, Feminists for Life actually devote most of their time and energy to college women, so you'll pretty much always encounter them on campuses.

They have two goals when it comes to college women:

1. Convince them to turn their nose up at real feminism.

2. Beg of them to consider the advantages of giving birth while in college, which totally will not cramp your style if you hand over your healthy white infant to some middle-class couple who would go wanting if you selfishly refused to play incubator for them. However, they do offer some hazy support, with very little real action behind it, in getting daycare for you. Or perhaps a wedding certificate so you can make the good little wifey for that poor, suffering frat boy you hoped you'd never have to see again. Don't be a snob. Surely he has good genes to give your baby.

CLAIM TO FEMINISM

Feminists for Life prefer to lay claim to feminism in the same way that all conservatives lay claim to progressive movements they want to co-opt, which is to find some dead progressive leaders and claim to be speaking for them. One favorite conservative line is to claim that for some reason Martin Luther King Jr. would oppose affirmative action. Their main evidence for this is that he, being dead, can't talk back, now can he?

In the same vein, Feminists for Life argue that they are the true keepers of the feminist flame because surely leaders of the women's suffrage movement, who are all also conveniently dead, would be appalled by abortion rights. They do back up their case with some industrious and extremely selective quote-mining, cobbling together at least five or six highly edited and decontextualized quotes from suffragists that indicate some discomfort with abortion as it was practiced in the nineteenth century, when it had a good chance of killing a woman. Needless to say, five or six quotes out of context is hardly the substantial background required to lay claim to a few hundred years of activism, so Feminists for Life has a backup plan.

CLAIM TO FEMINISM, PART TWO

Feminists for Life, aware that quote-mining suffragists is hardly evidence of being feminist, have attempted to find some policy measures that are feminist enough to give them credibility. Since many feminist goals like universal daycare have the pleasant side effect of reducing the need for abortion, Feminists for Life hitch their wagon to these policy proposals and hope that works to distract people from the fact that they are an organization dedicated primarily to the goal of passing laws against women's basic reproductive rights. To make the whole situation worse, since the primary members and funding sources of Feminists for Life are Republicans, their supposed support for things like universal daycare can safely be written off as all hat, no cattle. They simply aren't going to put massive pressure behind measures that will require increased social spending, especially since to do so would take precious time away from convincing white girls to make babies to give up for adoption.

WHAT TO DO IF YOU HAVE TO DEAL WITH THEM

If you have an opportunity to mess with Feminists for Life, which is likely if you're a college student, there's one great way to hammer at them, repeatedly. Like all pro-life organizations, Feminists for Life is opposed to increasing contraception access and education, which is the single best way to reduce abortion rates. Ask them at their tables or at the public forums they come to what they're doing to make sure that every woman who wants a condom or a pack of birth control pills has that. Ask them about their education outreach and whether or not they're fighting against things like abstinence-only education, which is linked to high abortion rates. For a group that claims to be all about reducing the need for abortion, Feminists for Life is shockingly unwilling to actually take measures that reduce the need for abortion. Asking them to explain why they won't do what they claim to do has a solid chance of exposing why they aren't the feminists they claim to be.

Feminists Who Are Not: The Miniskirt Edition

Ever hear anyone call Ann Coulter a feminist? Believe it or not, it happens. The miniskirt and the big mouth confuse people, for one thing. But for another, there's an entire subdivision of antifeminist reactionaries who try to pass themselves off as feminists, and this tends to muddy the waters and allow people to mistake Coulter for a feminist. It's a testament to the success of feminism that antifeminists actually try to co-opt our movement, but it's also incredibly galling. The most successful attempts at this have been perpetrated by a rough confederacy of antifeminist women who call themselves "i-feminists," which stands for "independent feminists," the implication being that real feminists are somehow dependent. On whom or what is up to the listener to decide, but presumably real feminists are not dependent on men, or else we'd be smiled upon warmly by i-feminists. Their other term for themselves is "equity feminists," but apparently they are not actually all in the lending professions.

I-feminists pass in the media as feminists because their shtick is to portray themselves as the only true defenders of real, old-fashioned feminism, what feminism was before feminists got their hands on it and destroyed it. The bible of i-feminism is *Who Stole Feminism?* by Christina Hoff Summers, which answers its own question by arguing that feminists stole feminism, possibly from those who were using feminism for its true calling of supporting and upholding male dominance. Camille Paglia and Wendy McElroy are the other bigwigs of i-feminism, and their main argument is that feminism has gotten far away from its original true calling of protecting date rapists in the name of equality.

So how can you tell that a woman who calls herself a feminist is in fact one of these "equity" feminists, i.e. Miniskirted Feminists Who Are Not? Well, they tend to have opinions that allow them to uphold male dominance while saying they believe in equality.

FEMINISTS SHOULDN'T FIGHT FOR ABORTION RIGHTS, BECAUSE WOMEN WHO GET ABORTIONS ARE LAZY AND DON'T DESERVE DEFENDERS

I-feminists technically believe in sexual and reproductive freedom, but for some reason they can't bring themselves to lift a finger actually defending these rights. Few will come right out and say they think abortion should be banned, but they have very little patience for those of us who defend abortion rights. "If you used birth control, you wouldn't need an abortion," is the usual refrain, and the retort to the reminder that contraception fails at times is simply incredulity that anything other than user error could result in contraceptive failure.

It hasn't yet been determined how "independence" would lead one to think that entire rights should just disappear because some of the people who use those rights may once have taken their birth control pill half a day late. We asked some equity feminists to explain themselves, but they made *pfft* sounds and rolled their eyes at the very idea that anyone could ever make an honest mistake that led to an accidental pregnancy.

FEMINISTS WHO FIGHT AGAINST DATE RAPE JUST HAVE SOMETHING AGAINST SEX OR MEN

This is a big one. I-feminist Katie Roiphe wrote an entire book called *The Morning After* that posits that rape victims are mainly just women who've had bad sex, and instead of acting like rational human beings and blowing it off, they decide to spend months and years making hay over it in the criminal justice system. Hell hath no fury like a woman who didn't get head, apparently.

The argument for coddling date rapists is that if women can't suffer a little rape here and there, then that makes us look weak and, that is Bad for Feminism. Legal and social remedies against date rape are very bad for date rapists too, but few i-feminists besides Camille Paglia will come out and say outright that the interests of feminists should align themselves with the interests of rapists.

FEMINISTS NEED TO BE MORE CONCERNED ABOUT THE SUFFERING OF BOYS AND MEN WHO HAVE TO COMPETE WITH WOMEN IN SCHOOL AND THE WORKPLACE NOW, THE POOR DEARS

This is one of the biggest new concerns of "equity" feminists, now that the evidence is pouring in that women and girls will hold their own with men in school and the workplace if given the same opportunities. This has created an outpouring of anguish that feminists are not giving enough of our time and energy to bolstering boys and men who are seeing their dominance languish for the first time in recorded history. The new enemy that i-feminists scold feminists about is the grave danger that is Title IX, a law that forces schools to give equal funding and access to boys and girls in school.

If a so-called feminist starts ranting about how equal access and funding are simply not fair to boys, then you've got yourself an "equity" feminist. Ask her why she thinks so little of boys that they have to be cushioned from competing with girls fairly. And if she actually comes up with an answer besides the usual i-feminist responses (accusing you of man-hating or rolling her eyes), well, you should trap her and keep her on display, because she's a rare beast.

And there's one last surefire way to tell that the so-called feminist you're dealing with is a Miniskirted Feminist Who Is Not:

DESPITE THE FACT THAT SHE CALLS HERSELF A FEMINIST, WHEN ACTUALLY ENGAGING WITH FEMINISTS, SHE WILL INEVITABLY GET CARRIED AWAY AND SAY "YOU FEMINISTS," AS IF "FEMINISTS" AND SHE ARE MUTUALLY EXCLUSIVE

Which they are.

In general, "equity feminists" are the antifeminists who are most fond of pushing the idea that real feminists are man-haters, and particularly that we hate sex. But there's another batch of fake feminists that prefers the other stereotype of real feminists, the erroneous belief that we are just professional sluts whose only political motivation is to have legal assistance in being even sluttier than we already are.

Fighting the Real Oppression — "Men's Rights Activists"

One of the most comical expressions of the Angry White Male syndrome is the formation of political groups claiming to fight the oppression of men by the feminist cabal. From groups like Fathers 4 Justice to popular websites, men's rights activism is on the move, and utterly delusional in every step of its journey. The basic theory of men's rights activism goes as such:

- Women totally got full equality sometime in the mid-'60s. The exact date is hard to pin, but generally it was prior to *Roe v. Wade*. (While not all Men's Rights Activists are antichoice, pretty much all believe that legalized abortion gave women more rights than men. They refuse to acknowledge that men have the exact same rights to abort their pregnancies as women.)
- Since women were completely equal forty years ago, the persistent existence of feminism must indicate that feminists are actually out to get men.
- The feminist conspiracy against men is to blame for all men's problems in life, from the divorce to traffic to their favorite team losing the playoffs.

The vast majority of MRAs have had a bitter divorce at some point, and most of their divorces were bitter because they refused to accept the fact that their marriages were over and move on, instead choosing to sue their wives repeatedly, first for custody of the children, then to reduce child support, then to get some itemized invoice detailing how the child support is spent, then to prevent their ex-wife from moving or getting remarried. Then, when all those options are tapped out, some of them start getting creative and start suing to stop their ex-wives from smoking or saying bad words. It's for the children, of course. Of the small minority who aren't divorced, the vast majority of them are Nice Guys who are embittered because the women they date keep insisting on having sexually unappealing attributes like their own opinions.

How can you tell the asshole you're dealing with is probably a card-carrying MRA? Mention a mail-order bride service. If he starts ranting about how American women are spoiled and selfish, and how women from impoverished, war-torn countries really know how to treat a man, you have yourself an MRA. If he starts taking bride-hunting trips to the former Soviet states, alert the immigration authorities.

MRAs only have a handful of issues they obsess over, and they are rather telling.

DOMESTIC VIOLENCE AGAINST WOMEN IS NOT AN ISSUE

MRAs deny, in turns, that domestic violence is common, and when they will admit it's common, they'll claim women do it just as much. The evidence that women are "just as bad" comes from the theory that if a guy bruises his knuckles on your face, you've both sustained a domestic violence injury. Therefore, they argue that shelters for women should let in men, which would be a great help to men seeking out their wives who are trying to flee them. Apparently, if women don't want their violent husbands to pretend to be suffering themselves in order to find and pursue them, those women shouldn't have gotten themselves beaten, or possibly, they shouldn't have wanted to escape.

RAPE ISN'T A PROBLEM, BUT THE HORDES OF WOMEN LYING ABOUT RAPE ARE

The theory is that rape almost never happens. What happens is that women have sex with unappealing people, possibly after drinking too much, and they regret it to their cores. (For some reason, MRAs can easily imagine a woman regretting sex with someone so much that she wants to scrub her very skin off.) At this point, to go along with their story, you have to remember that in their world, women aren't human so much as alien beings. At this point, the woman doesn't sneak out in the morning and try to pretend it never happened, and maybe even drives home the point by refusing to acknowledge her regretted lover in public.

No, in the MRA world, what your average woman does at this point is file rape charges. Because there's no better way in the world to get over a one-night stand than to have to rehash it to police, then detectives, then to a prosecutor, then to a grand jury, and then to a trial jury. And nothing preserves your sexual reputation so much as having a defense lawyer dig up every guy you've ever kissed and go over them at trial in lurid detail in order to make you sound like the biggest slut on the planet.

Then again, most MRAs voted for a guy who promised that the best way to get rid of terrorism was to bomb a country the terrorists weren't even in. So this story makes sense in their world.

CHILD SUPPORT IS THE GREATEST SOCIAL ILL THE WORLD HAS EVER KNOWN

To be fair, some of them simply skip this step and wish out loud that women couldn't file for divorce, but the general sentiment is the same. If a woman isn't in your house sucking your cock and cleaning your floors, then why the hell should you give her money? The argument that one should take care of one's children tends to fall on deaf ears. The anger about child support has grown to the point that MRAs commonly claim that women date men strictly to get married to them, live with them and raise a couple of children, and then divorce them—all for that money train of $300 to $800 a month, which is usually less than half of what a woman's paying to keep up the children.

The most common strategy for making sure that no woman who isn't sucking your dick or cleaning your floors gets a dime of your money is to sue for joint custody. Often, this doesn't work, because men who are this sexist have often left all the child-rearing predivorce to their wives, and judges rightfully wonder why a man with no previous interest in his children suddenly cares now. But in MRA-land, judges, who are on average middle-aged white men, are all in cahoots with Gloria Steinem to take their money.

IF MEN TREAT WOMEN AS SEX OBJECTS, THEN WOMEN TREAT MEN AS "SUCCESS OBJECTS"

It's hard to deny that if you're a man, having money is a good step toward getting more dates. That said, it's a little ripe for MRAs to complain one minute that women in America are materialists, only after money, and then solve their supposed problems by traveling to countries where they know that the women are so impoverished that putting up with asshole husbands in order to get a green card starts looking like a good deal.

SITCOMS ARE OFTEN LESS THAN FLATTERING TOWARD MEN

While this seems to be an odd complaint, it's in the top five MRA reasons men are oppressed. Granted, they are working with pretty lean material in drafting their grievances, so it's understandable that this is the best they can come up with. The general complaint is that men on sitcoms are portrayed as daft morons contrasted with their hypercompetent wives. Unmentioned is that said men are often portrayed also as fat slobs, contrasted with wives who look like they just stepped off the pages of *Vogue*.

One could say that the reason this happens is because the standard comedic setup is a straight man vs. a funny man, and the funny man is, because he's funny, usually some combination of ill-kempt, stupid, and cranky. One could also point out that the straight man—kept on hand to contrast with the funny man—is usually everything the funny man is not, which is well-kept, straitlaced, competent, and even-tempered. While the straight man is more socially acceptable in the real world, in the entertainment world, the funny man gets all the accolades for delivering the laughs. One classic example is Grace, as the funny man, vs. George, her straight man. Or Lucy the funny man vs. Ricky, her straight man.

If you buy the *crazy* notion that the funny man is the real star of the sitcom, then suddenly it might taint your view of men on sitcoms as the unkempt laugh-line deliverers vs. their wives who are mostly there to look good and be the straight men. You might think these shows are built around the male leads and meant to make the men the stars of the show. You might start to think that the fact that women are never the stars is another example of how we still live in a male-dominated society.

And you'd be wrong in the MRA world, of course. We build the evidence around the theory. That sitcom stars are predominantly men is just more evidence that women secretly rule the world, and asking further questions only indicates your complicity with the feminist conspiracy.

Ladies' Night: The Final Frontier in Equality

hip Rowe calls it the "curious campaign against free booze for girls," which is as good a description as any of the weirdest offshoot of antifeminist attempts to rewrite reality to confirm the odd belief that not only is there widespread discrimination against men, but there's also a feminist conspiracy to conceal said discrimination. At his website (www.chiprowe.com) and in the December 2003 edition of *Playboy*, Chip made a long list of various legal battles waged by men who are determined to end gender inequality by attacking the only instance of it they seem to see, which is in the area of women getting discounts on alcohol that men are not getting on a whole night or two a week at a handful of nightclubs in any major urban center. Starting in 1979, and up until he wrote the article in 2003, Rowe recorded twelve separate lawsuits against clubs that offered discounted drinks or club admission for women on the theory that women would come for the discounts, and men for the women.

It seems that if one expects women to pay full price for drinks, one would also agitate to make sure women make as much as men in order to pay those full prices, but alas, these male warriors against gender inequality feel that inequality begins and ends at the cash register of the local watering hole. Moreover, they seem very angry that feminists have not taken the time to address the horrible inequality that is Ladies' Night, instead wasting our time on issues like employment discrimination and the right to obtain full medical care whether one has a uterus or not. Feminist unwillingness to divert resources to stopping the horrible injustice of Ladies' Night is often held up as damning evidence that feminists are not interested in equality at all, but are actually conspiring against men to make sure men pay more for alcohol.

It's cruel to view these male warriors against Ladies' Night as nothing more than assholes with bizarre notions of how the world works. Or, as some have insinuated, as men who are mostly angry that they can't even get laid hitting on someone so drunk off twenty-five-cent well drinks that Ron Jeremy looks like Jude Law.

No, I prefer to be generous and see these men as what they are: the fabled man and sex-hating feminists we hear so much about. You know the ones I'm talking about—the legendary feminists who think that heterosexual intercourse is the cornerstone of all gender inequality and who therefore prioritize stomping out heterosexual intercourse in most, if not all, of its manifestations. Said feminists look askance on any and all male attempts to get laid, though some of them might be mildly accepting of heterosexual sex, so long as it's within a thoroughly respectful, monogamous, egalitarian relationship, and even then, it has to happen without anything resembling objectifying behavior. Most of us hear a lot about these feminists, but never see them. Turns out we're looking in the wrong place. Those feminists are the all-male Ladies' Night opposition.

After all, what is Ladies' Night if not the embodiment of the very sexified culture that these mostly mythological radical feminists hate? The whole thing is based around bribing women to parade around in front of men who are objectifying them and often seeking to physically penetrate them at some point in time. Anyone stepping in to stop the bribery, the objectification of women for male pleasure, and the meaningless sexual intercourse—and more importantly, stopping it in the name of gender equality—is bound to be one of those radical feminists you hear so much about. Who knew they'd turn out to be not only men, but also men who generally seem to have a grudge against feminism?

Playboy Fantasy

ugh Hefner's vision for his readers—a shared fantasy where men are erudite playboys enamored of their own intelligence and sensual pleasures while women are all nubile fuckholes with no minds, needs, or threatening desires outside of the desire to pay rapt attention to their masculine keepers—is shocking not so much in that it existed, or even that it sold magazines, but that anyone ever actually bought into it. Not that most readers of *Playboy* did buy into the "philosophy," of course. Most of them bought into the idea that seeing pictures of naked women was an enjoyable thing. But there were some who bought into the whole package, even though they are a dying breed. Hefner himself has exposed the lie by turning his life into a reality show where viewers get to see how intellectual he and his most definitely are not.

Research, however, has demonstrated that the *Playboy* fanboys haven't so much disappeared as morphed into a new, even more irritating beast: libertarians. At first blush, it hardly seems possible, since the old *Playboy* fans presumably loved silk pajamas, martinis, and reading actual literature, whereas those who call themselves libertarians love boxer shorts, beer and pot, and reading Ayn Rand. How could have things shifted so much, so quickly? It's hard to say, but idiot-watchers are inclined to blame the advent of video games as the main culprit. Outside of that, the two populations have much in common.

PSEUDOINTELLECTUALISM

In the first issue of *Playboy*, Hefner set the eyeroll-provoking tone. "We like our apartment. We enjoy mixing up cocktails and an hors d'oeuvre or two, putting a little mood music on the phonograph, and inviting in a female acquaintance for a quiet discussion on Picasso, Nietzsche, jazz, sex." In this same way, libertarians try to repackage their egos in such a way that they seem to have some intellectual justification for themselves, particularly with their love of Rand's pseudophilosophy of Objectivism. For what it's worth, Rand was, like Hugh Hefner, a fan of overwrought prose without a hint of self-awareness. "My philosophy, in essence, is the concept of man as a heroic being, with his own happiness as the moral purpose of his life, with productive achievement as his noblest activity, and reason as his only absolute." (From the appendix to *Atlas Shrugged*.)

DOTH PROTESTING TOO MUCH

One reason that Hefner is embarrassing is that he doesn't seem to get that he wouldn't be fucking four eighteen-year-olds a night if he weren't paying through the nose for the pleasure. What's worse is anyone who can't pay for that pleasure looking up to him. In the same vein, your average libertarian tends to be a loud defender of certain pleasures that one doubts he actually gets to enjoy much, with the one exception of pot-smoking. Not that there's anything wrong with defending liberty to pursue pleasures, but there's something peculiarly libertarian about talking up sodomy and then hitting a joint and enjoying the liberty of World of Warcraft.

BADLY CONCEALED HOSTILITY TOWARD WOMEN

One of the best moments in all of blogging history was when a popular libertarian blogger named Libertarian Girl was outed as . . . a man. When the blogger was outed, he noted, "One thing I learned from this blog is how easy attractive women have it. When I had a blog as my real self, no one linked to me, no one left any comments, it was as if the blog existed in a vacuum. But things were different for Libertarian Girl. Every day I'd check Technorati and discover new unsolicited links." He was only half-right about it being easier for attractive women than men to get attention. It's a lot easier for attractive women to get attention if they exist in an environment almost devoid of women and are willing to hear loser after loser tell them how superior to other women they are. In other words, it's easier for an attractive woman to get by as a libertarian if she's actually a man in disguise.

Playboy lovers claim to love women, and they do love them—in two dimensions and airbrushed.

SELF-DELUSION

Playboy's true believers want to make jerking off seem like it's something more interesting than it is. Libertarians want to vote Republican without having to actually be Republicans, because they correctly perceive how deeply uncool conservatives are. What they fail to grasp is they're only cooler than Republicans in the sense that Rush is marginally cooler than Lawrence Welk.

WANKERY

Not just the kind you'd expect (not that I would criticize that kind of wanking in a book that also praises the uses and abuses of vibrating devices made for women). There's something wankerish about fantasizing about one's self being catered to by nubile women while wearing silk pajamas and listening to jazz one probably doesn't even like. Similarly, there's something incredibly wankerish about fantasizing that if the big, mean government just got out of your way, you'd be like a king or something, living in a castle with a passel of nubile women who use you for protection, due to the large weapons cache you've built up to protect yourself in this policeless world.

HOW TO AVOID BOTH *PLAYBOY* FANBOYS AND LIBERTARIANS

Tell 'em you're a feminist. While it's something of a stereotype and certainly not true across the board, feminists tend to have a reputation for being genuinely intelligent and impatient with bullshit. Both of these things are kryptonite toward both *Playboy* fanboys and libertarians.

One small disclaimer: Whenever I make fun of libertarians, I invariably have a couple of old-fashioned left-libertarians complain that not all libertarians fit the popular image of the wanker libertarian. So a word of caution that there are still some left-libertarians who hang on to the word "libertarian," even though it's been thoroughly claimed by the wankers.

When Sexism Isn't Sexism: The Pay Gap

I may be an oddball in this regard, but as a general rule, I don't dedicate brain cells to remembering the names of the various presidents of Ivy League universities. Despite this well-reasoned preference for saving those brain cells for more compelling information, such as the names of minor characters on *Buffy the Vampire Slayer*, I was compelled eventually to remember the name of Larry Summers, once the president of Harvard and now a martyr to the cause of people who really, really want to be able to claim women are naturally stupid on a regular basis.

Summers got into a pickle by claiming that the reason more women weren't succeeding in numbers as high as men in math and science positions was, in part, due to women's lesser abilities. Naturally, this irritated some of the female scientists in the room, for roughly the same reason that it's irritating to have your half-literate uncle tell you that women are simply less smart than men while you're polishing your Phi Beta Kappa key. Which is not to say that Summers is stupid, but it's ill advised to tell female scientists that women are less adept at science for scientific reasons when you are not a scientist.

But Summers was a man, and his detractors were either women or traitors to the asshole male cause, so the half-literate uncles of the world immediately sprung into action defending him. Unfortunately, many half-literate uncles have highly paid jobs at conservative think tanks, and have frequent opportunities to hold forth on their opinions in Rupert Murdoch–financed media sources and the *Wall Street Journal*. It set off a new round of the argument that sexism isn't sexism, and that women who don't move up in fields where their bosses might, like Summers, tend to believe women are less capable only have their own dim-wittedness to blame. And most of the after-the-fact apologias for a sexist system argued that the 20 to 25 percent smaller salary that women make on average is not a problem and is not caused by sexism at all.

The argument has become so ossified that many of the people making it neglect to realize they're arguing that there's no such thing as sexism by referring to sexist practices. So if you hear someone bloviating about how the pay gap isn't caused by sexism, here are the arguments you are likely to hear:

WOMEN AVOID MALE-DOMINATED FIELDS LIKE ENGINEERING OR CONSTRUCTION WORK

This is considered evidence against sexism because at some point, a voluntary choice to avoid these jobs was made. Sure, it's a voluntary choice made after sizing up the involuntary obstacles such as the hostility you'll get as a woman trying to push yourself into a boys' club. The argument works if you refuse to consider male hostility, and even outright sexual harassment, as sexism.

WOMEN PUT IN FEWER HOURS AT WORK THAN MEN DO

According to Steve Chapman, writing for *Reason Online* in May 2007, the pay gap can be explained away in part because men will work fifty hours a week and women will only work forty. This is not sexism, so long as you buy into the assumption that sexism has nothing to do with the fact that women need to make time at home to clean toilets and cook hamburgers, while men can easily cut into their sitcom-watching time to get ahead at the office.

WOMEN QUIT THEIR JOBS TO WATCH CHILDREN WHILE MEN DON'T

With the handy trick of redefining sexism as not-sexism, this argument also works perfectly to show how the pay gap between men and women can be chalked up to not-sexism. Staying home to watch the children and being dependent on your husband is often defended vigorously as a choice that has no relationship whatsoever to sexism. Most of the time, you can shut down people defending the choice to stay home as one made independent of sexist pressures by asking them why men keep finding other pursuits—golf, late hours at the office, second wives—rather than making the choice to drop out of the rat race completely and become full-time stay-at-home dads, if that choice is so damn appealing and not made under sexist pressure. So far, a good answer to this question has not been recorded.

WOMEN PREFER SOFT, NONTHREATENING JOBS THAT EMPHASIZE THEIR CUTER, MORE FEMININE SIDES

People apologizing for the pay gap like to point out how women find themselves preferring jobs where they'll get praised for filling their gender roles of nurturing others, such as teaching and social work, and avoiding jobs where they run the high risk of being called ball-busting bitches. While it might seem as if widespread social stereotypes that wedge women out of higher-paying careers and into lower-paying ones could possibly be called "sexist," through the careful use of hand-waving and the heavy application of the word "choice," you can magically transform the gender divisions between women's lower-paid careers and men's higher-paid careers from sexism to not-sexism.

WHEN ALL THE CHIPS ARE DOWN, THE FINAL ARGUMENT IS THAT WOMEN ARE LESS CAPABLE

As the Larry Summers controversy shows, nothing is considered better evidence that sexism is not a factor in the pay gap than making blatantly sexist comments about women's inabilities. Sexism thereby turns itself into not-sexism by pointing out that sexism is only the natural reaction to sexism-provoking imbecile females, who are not good for anything but typing vigorously and raising children.

With all this not-sexism contributing to the pay gap, it's hard not to wonder what it would take for something to be considered actual sexism to apologists for the pay gap. Once you eliminate the second shift, the pressure to stay home, the pressure not to compete in male-dominated fields, and the assumption that women are less capable, what you have left is the image of some evil boss man twirling his mustache at a bright, young, innocent female job applicant and saying to her, "But my dear, we don't hire women here, since we are dues-paying members of the Sexist Conspiracy."

Once upon a time, there was an American president. He was a Democrat, and when he entered office, the country had not had a Democrat as president for twelve years. And it was found out shortly after he entered office that many people had believed during that twelve years that there would never be another Democratic president, and they were very angry. By most measures, this president was moderately conservative, but to the angry people, it made no difference. In their eyes, he was a Marxist through and through and had to be destroyed. Lies were told and scandals were manufactured, but nothing worked.

And then one day the president received a blowjob from one of the White House interns, a forward young lady with dark hair and a fondness for Gap clothing. Thus the Clenis was born, springing fully formed from Kenneth Starr's briefcase.

The Clenis and its awesome power was best defined by the blog Corrente:

Abbrev. The Mighty Member of the Big Dog, our last elected president: The Cl[inton P]enis.

Who could begin to define a signifier of such mighty power?

The Clenis is worth about $10 million per inch as measured by the Republicans investigating it. . . . And to hear the Republicans tell it, The Clenis is responsible for everything that's wrong with the country, then and now. . . . Watch them shift the subject to The Clenis whenever they start losing an argument on the merits; it's fun!

The Clenis was named by a commenter named Jennifer in the comment section of the blog Eschaton. The Clenis is used as an amulet by conservatives to ward off encroaching liberalism, much like a cross is used to fend off vampires. Whenever a conservative finds himself on the losing end of an argument, he brandishes the Clenis, declares rhetorical victory, and walks off. Unless a liberal is willing to defend the Clenis to the death, then nothing else she says will ever count for anything. Atrios, the blogger at Eschaton, explains its function as "[a]n uncontrollable urge to blurt out 'Clinton did it!' or 'Oh yeah? What about Clinton?' rather than using logic and reason to make one's point."

The Clenis functions against liberals in general, but it's a favorite tactic to shut up feminists. Despite the fact that Bill Clinton was as supportive of feminist causes as one could expect from a conservative Democrat, many conservatives treat his affair with Monica Lewinsky as a trump card over considerations like policy and women's rights. The Clenis rejoinder stipulates that all feminists everywhere who take understandable discomfort with a sexual relationship between the president and a much younger intern (one that was nonetheless consensual by any measure) should quit offering Clinton support, and while we're at it, withdraw our political support for his wife, his friends, anyone who ever worked with him, and anyone who shares a political party with him.

That this would require abstention from voting or voting only for Republicans is treated like an unfortunate side effect, though some people suspect that it's the main purpose of invoking the Clenis on feminists. Refraining from disavowing any support for Clinton is grounds for having your status as a good feminist revoked by the conservative who yanked out the Clenis.

Political blogger and occasional *New York Times* op-ed writer Ann Althouse is known in particular for her promiscuous brandishing of the Clenis. Most notoriously, she attacked prominent feminist Jessica Valenti for meeting Bill Clinton at a lunch and having her picture taken with him, demanding that no good feminist would do such a thing. In a blog post where she derided Valenti for her lunch meeting, the law-professor-*cum*-blogger noted that the sexual magnetism of the Clenis was such that the meeting must have been arranged for sexual reasons, writing, "Then, when she goes to meet Clinton, she wears a tight knit top that draws attention to her breasts and stands right in front of him and positions herself to make her breasts as obvious as possible?"

People not enraptured by the power of the Clenis didn't perceive Valenti as wearing a tight top or sticking her tits in the former president's face, but otherwise the insinuation seemed grounded. The lunch was, after all, organized by Bill Clinton's wife's campaign staff. Why wouldn't Hillary Clinton dedicate campaign resources toward funneling potential girlfriends to her husband? But by the time you've been sucked into asking these questions, the Clenis trump card has worked. You've started to play into the game where the presidential penis is treated as more important than the actual issues.

WHAT TO DO WHEN CONFRONTED WITH THE CLENIS

Prepare yourself ahead of time. You simply cannot live in denial and believe that no one will flash the Clenis at you. A trump card that can derail any discussion about the issues into a finger-pointing session on who is the biggest adultery-coddler is too great a temptation for the weak wills of many wingnuts, particularly those of an antifeminist bent. You may have avoided it in the past, but it will crop up one day—from the loudmouthed college Republican in your poli-sci class, from your right-wing relatives when you go home to visit, from your lover's boorish brother-in-law who thinks he's clever because he listens to talk radio, or from some spastic wingnut on an Internet discussion board. And it will almost always seem like it's out of left field, because "out of left field" is its nature.

You: Well, the problems with the Iraq War go back to when the Bush administration lied about weapons of mass des—
Clenis-Flasher: Well, Clinton lied about a blow job!

Or

You: And so we should implement this sexual harassment program so that victims have a confidential way to report inci—

Clenis-Flasher: Did you feel that way when Clinton was getting a blow job?

Or

You: So this new car I got actually gets forty-six miles to the gal—

Clenis-Flasher: Boy, if Clinton hadn't got that blowjob, his butt boy Gore would be in office and we'd all have to be hippies like you.

Your first reaction will most likely be "stunned." Don't be ashamed—when someone flashes his Clenis at you, it's natural to be appalled at the tastelessness, and, more importantly, the senselessness, of it all. But you can recover and smack down the flasher.

APOLOGIZE FOR THE FAILINGS OF FEMINISM THAT LED TO CLINTON'S LONG-AGO ADULTERY

Suggested wording: "We feminists do feel terrible about what happened. We weren't aware at the time that Clinton's penis was our responsibility. We've rectified that mistake with our new policy of putting a tracker in the pants of every new president. You don't really want to know what Bush does with his, but let's just say that I never knew that some families keep a pair of tongs by the toilet."

TAKE PERSONAL RESPONSIBILITY FOR CLINTON'S UNFAITHFULNESS

"Yes, I voted for Clinton. I foolishly thought it better to have a good president with a messy personal life that's none of my business than a president who, while seemingly clean-living, would get us into wars and strip away women's rights."

ADMIT THAT SUPPORT FOR A POLITICIAN WITH FEMINIST POLICIES IS DEEPLY UNFEMINIST

"Sure, marital fidelity is not really a political issue to feminists, and sure, one would think that feminists have a right to judge their politicians by their own standards rather than by the ones that hostile parties demand. But you've told me that feminism is about enforcing the marital vow and not about women's political and social rights at all. So I guess I have to go with that."

AGREE THAT CLINTON WAS THE WORST THING THAT EVER HAPPENED TO WOMEN'S RIGHTS

"Sure, there's no reason to think that having a consensual sexual relationship is evidence of sexual harassment, but in this particular case, the strenuous application of right-wing magic and millions of dollars of taxpayer money almost made that true. Which then hurt women's rights more than anything that the Republicans could do, up to and including actually passing laws taking away women's rights. The only rights that really count are the imaginary ones that were hurt when Clinton got some head—not the rights enjoyed by living, breathing women."

AGREE THAT CLINTON IS A BAD ROLE MODEL

"From what I understand from all the angry articles, Clinton actually managed to invent oral sex. If nothing else, he made the world a sadder place for that. It's going to take a lot of misleading abstinence-only scare tactics in the classroom to make up for the damage done to the stick shoved up our nation's collective ass."

By this point in time, you will should have conceded enough points that your conservative opponent will be begging you to quit, but if that hasn't happened yet, add one more concession.

SUGGEST THAT OUR COUNTRY'S POOR INTERNATIONAL REPUTATION IS THE FAULT OF THE CLENIS

"Some might say that America's slipshod reputation around the world is Bush's fault, especially with the thousands of people who have died needlessly because of his war, and with international policies like the global gag rule. Those people are crazy. I think it's because people didn't realize you could cheat on your spouse before Clinton showed them it was possible. Internationally, things have gone downhill since then."

Or, if you're not in the mood to concede a bunch of random points up front, you could insist on staying on topic. Good luck with that. Odds are your Clenis-flasher will assume you're evading the issue, and that deep down inside, you're just scared of the Clenis.

A Covenful of Girl Scouts

Growing paranoia about the feminist threat to our nation has led many a right-wing nut to see feminist bogeywimmin in every corner. Of all their targets as suspected feminist threats, however, my favorite has got to be the Girl Scouts. Before, they were known as just a threat to dieters with their cookie-pushing ways, but now the Girl Scouts are seen as a feminist-propaganda training camp by groups such as Concerned Women for America, whose former president Robert Knight argued in 2005 that the Girl Scouts promote abortion and lesbianism. His main issue with the Scouts is that they book pro-woman speakers like Kavita Ramdas, president and CEO of the Global Fund for Women, as keynote speakers at their conventions. Ramdas's big sin in the eyes of the CWA was her willingness to support women's reproductive rights. Clearly, booking speakers who care about what happens to little girls as they grow into actual women is a sign that the Girl Scouts have fallen into the clutches of man-hating radical feminists.

In honor of this occasion, I've put together some suggestions for the new merit badges for these radical, man-hating, feminist cookie dealers.

SPELL-CASTING. TEN HOURS.

Learn all the latest spells from Satan himself, and grow up to be the leader of your own coven! Spells you must accomplish in order to successfully finish your ten hours: Love Spells (better to control men), Impotence Spells, and Mind Control Spells.

DO-IT-YOURSELF ABORTIONS. THREE HOURS.

To achieve this merit badge, you must learn how to kill your best friend's husband's baby while it's still in the womb with nothing more than a coat hanger and a bottle of whiskey. (Must be postpuberty to achieve this badge.)

NAGGING. FIVE HOURS.

A must-have badge for our weaker-minded Girl Scouts who would dare marry a man. Learn how to drive a man insane with your constant demands. Topics covered: I Want Sexual Satisfaction Too, Why Don't You Pull Your Weight Around Here, They're Your Children Too.

BRA-BURNING. TWO HOURS.

Girls learn more than just how to wave a lighter under their bras and toss them in trash cans. This badge requires the scout to find all sorts of objects to set on fire, from copies of *Maxim* magazine to Barbie dolls to humble, dog-eared copies of *The Joy of Cooking*. Bonus points to girls who can come up with creative ways to throw off the shackles of the patriarchy in the most pyromaniacal ways possible.

TRICKING A MAN OUT OF HIS HARD-EARNED MONEY. THREE HOURS.

A girl's gotta make a living and there's no better way than to get on that $300-to $500-a-month child, support gravy train. To finish the requirements for this merit badge, you have to learn to seduce a man so that he has no ability to say no or even suggest the use of contraception. Then you learn how to secure a lawyer and get the entire court system on your side. The Spell-Casting Badge is a prerequisite.

EMASCULATION. TWO HOURS.

A radical feminist's favorite form of entertainment. Skills learned: Mean-spirited rejection, laughing in a man's face, disagreeing in public, telling embarrassing stories behind a man's back, snottily refusing to have the door opened for you, making decisions without consulting your husband.

CASTRATION. THREE HOURS.

Not for the faint of heart. To earn this merit badge, you must successfully learn the multiple techniques for separating a man from his genitals. Some techniques are more gruesome than others. The Emasculation Badge is a prerequisite.

Asshole-Bleaching: The New Frontier

The day I knew things had officially gone too far was on July 11, 2005, when I read this, by Tristan Taormino, in the *Village Voice:*

> *"Is there any way of making my anus more pink or lighter in color? Mine is dark and I hate it. Any suggestions?" I received this question from a female reader of my Anal Advisor column in Taboo, and believe it or not, she's not the only one pining for a pinker pucker. I've gotten letters from dozens of people asking how to make their buttholes better looking. Until recently, I couldn't give them much help, because based on my research, no product or procedure existed to lighten that place, which spends a lot of time in the dark. Then, this year, an episode of Dr. 90210 on E! featured porn star Tabitha Stevens visiting a salon in the San Fernando Valley to get her asshole bleached.*

At which point I stopped and had an existential crisis. Sure, we feminists have done many great things with our activism. We've won the vote, gotten women educated, gotten them jobs, helped them have a better family life, taught them that the clitoris is their friend and their lover's friend too. But we have somehow failed to stop the growing trend of asshole bleaching. In fact, this trend sprung up many years after the second wave of feminism and has managed to grow, despite the fact that we now live in a world where you don't have to get your asshole bleached if your husband asks, because you can leave him and get a real job.

If you ever find yourself lying on a table in a salon with your bare ass perched up toward the fluorescent lighting, and some nice lady who dreams of being a movie star one day is scooping bleach in between your ass cheeks, it's high time to consider whether you maybe have hit rock bottom in your addiction to prostrating yourself before the beauty myth.

Asshole-bleaching exposes how the beauty industry makes up a problem in order to fix it and separate you from your cash. I, for one, was not aware that assholes are not particularly pink or pearly, in no small part because I had never devoted a moment's thought to the grave issue that is The Color of Assholes (outside of considering the leadership of the Republican party, in which the color of assholes is white). Well, I never devoted a moment's thought until I read about asshole-bleaching. Apparently, assholes on white women tend toward the brown color, in one of those neat coincidences in nature where the symbol matches the function.

There seem to be only two major paths that lead a woman from relative sanity to asshole-bleaching. Either you get it in your head that your asshole needs to be a few shades lighter all on your lonesome, or some asshole in your life determines that your asshole in your pants could use a thick application of burning bleach. In either situation, the solution to your problems is not to bleach your asshole. In the latter case, tell the asshole that if he's close enough to see your asshole, the proper behavior is to appreciate the situation instead of bitterly wondering why you come with human parts instead of plastic parts.

If it's the former situation, there are many opportunities to stop and take stock of your situation. When you're kneeling on the bathroom sink, trying to aim your ass at the mirror so you can get a good look at the color of your asshole, that's a good time to stop and think, "Isn't there anything better I could be doing with my time?" If you're squatting over a handheld mirror in the bathroom—and it's not to participate in *Our Bodies, Ourselves*–style vaginal appreciation—that's a good time to say, "How does the color of my asshole matter at all to anyone, ever?"

With enough practice, you will probably find yourself moving beyond the urge to bleach your asshole. Once you've shrugged off this beauty myth pressure, it might be time to move up toward questioning why you need to spend $25 to have your eyebrows waxed so that they look exactly the same as if you'd spent two minutes on them with a pair of three-dollar tweezers (that can be reused, even).

Part 7.

IT'S NOT A POSTFEMINIST WORLD WHEN WE HAVE A LONG WAY TO GO

Is PETA the Same As Operation Rescue?

Feminists, pro-feminists, feminist allies, and assorted liberals—do not give money to PETA. Please. Someone is still giving them money, and it has to stop. I say this as a vegetarian environmentalist animal lover who openly has argued that a cat has more right to life than a fetus. (Due to the conscious-thought/ability-to-suffer factor.) Sometimes I think that PETA's funding and tactics indicate that they're actually a front for the meat industry to discredit vegetarians, but I know that's not so, because their tactics and philosophy come from the dark place in the human heart that also produces antichoicers. There are just too many similarities not to notice.

THEY THINK GROSSING YOU OUT IS AN ARGUMENT

Protests consisting of people waving bloody fetus pictures, and protests consisting of people waving bloody meat pictures are indistinguishable on the surface. The implication is that bad people turn cute things into bloody things, but there's no argument as to why this should be morally wrong, much less why it should be illegal.

THEY THINK WOMEN ARE JUST BODIES TO BE MANIPULATED FOR POLITICAL ENDS, INSTEAD OF FULL HUMAN BEINGS

Antichoicers see women, particularly young, fertile women, and they think, "Baby incubators." PETA sees women, particularly young, fertile women, and they think, "Bodies to undress in order to nab attention for our 'cause.'"

BOTH EXPLOIT TENDER YOUNG WOMEN AS CHEAP LABOR

Antichoice groups are notorious for mining fresh-faced teenage girls from church youth groups to put at the front of their marches for photo opportunities, as if to convey the message that they can't be that bad if the very people they want to hurt the most (women of childbearing age) are willing to stand by them. That, and it gives their mostly male leadership wank fodder. PETA notoriously recruits on college campuses in order to snag crunchy young women, most of whom are inclined to be feminists, before these women grow up enough to realize that just because a group claims to support animal welfare doesn't mean it's a group that pro-animal people want to associate themselves with.

BOTH PREFER TO ADVOCATE FOR "VICTIMS" THAT ARE SILENT AND THEREFORE CAN BE PROJECTED ONTO

It's no coincidence that people who are bereft of arguments and prefer sentimental whining and shock tactics prefer causes where the supposed victims are not able to articulate their own desires. Animals/fetuses give them their excuse to work out all sorts of other feelings, and not just disgust and anger toward female bodies, though that seems to be part of it.

BOTH HAVE A STRONG, IRRATIONAL LOATHING FOR SCIENCE

Maybe they watched too many "mad scientist" movies in their youth, but antichoicers share with PETA members a belief that science is the enemy. Antichoicers have made a crusade out of attacking stem cell research, even though they claim to be pro-life, and the research has the potential to save many lives. PETA members have the same attitude about research on animals, which they dedicate much of their resources to stopping, even though boring old meat-eating (which they are also against, to be fair) absolutely causes way more animal pain, suffering, and death than scientific research ever could. The levels of hostility toward scientific research are way out of proportion to the perceived problem, which inclines one to wonder whether both PETA and antichoicers dislike scientists because rationality is offensive to them.

NEITHER SEEMS TO CARE AS MUCH ABOUT THE REAL-LIFE WELL-BEING OF THE OBJECTS OF THEIR ADVOCACY AS THEY CLAIM TO CARE

Antichoice groups uniformly oppose contraception and sex education, which are the only proven methods of reducing the abortion rate overall. PETA has an unsavory history of liberating research animals only to have them die from the stress of their liberation. In fact, they don't even need to die by accident—PETA puts down the animals they supposedly rescue. There are allegations that PETA kills 85 percent of the animals they take in. Mind you, those allegations come from the food industry, so take them with a grain of salt, but there is no doubt that PETA routinely kills animals.

If you've been giving money to PETA, I beg you to quit and turn your animal-charity dollar over to the SPCA, or preferably your local no-kill shelter, especially if they run a feral cat program that is catch-neuter-release, which has been shown to help curtail animal overpopulation better than catch-and-kill. Sure, it's not as sexy as donating to PETA, but since PETA's definition of "sexy" is to equate naked women with slabs of meat in the grocery store, in this case, "sexy" isn't all it's cracked up to be.

The Name Change Is No Longer Sexist, so Just Shut Up and Do It

One of the oldest and most long-standing symbolic battles of feminism has been against the assumption that women who marry men should automatically change their last names when they do so. Feminists fought long and hard to overturn laws mandating that wives be named after husbands and that children be named after fathers. The result of these long, hard battles is that you now have a right not to change your name when you marry, but that right will seem a small comfort if you do get engaged and suddenly you feel the pressure from all sides to conform to the name change. And it's an ugly pressure. There will be insinuations that you aren't committed to your husband. (How he shows commitment without changing his name is a question left to the gods.) There will be insinuations that you don't love your husband, or are plotting to run off with the pool boy after you get your hands on your husband's millions (or, if you're like most of us, after you get your hands on his ratty sofa and ten-year-old car). There will be insinuations that you intend to castrate your new husband in his sleep.

Odds are that you have the willpower to blow these sillier insinuations off. But be prepared, because the patriarchy-promoters have a new trick up their sleeve to convince the feminist bride that she must change her name, and that trick is to argue that there's nothing sexist about abandoning the name you've had your whole life to be Mrs. Somethingorother. No, there's now a whole roster of reasons that women should change their names when they marry that have nothing whatsoever to do with sexism, according to the defenders of the practice. Some of the most common:

WHAT ABOUT THE KIDS?

This one is most commonly voiced under the assumption that a woman who doesn't change her name will be the odd man out in her family in the surname department after she has kids. Even as people grasp the idea that women don't have to change their names when they marry, the assumption that children have to be named after their fathers persists. It makes sense if you assume that a father should be rewarded for the great effort of not pushing a baby out of a small hole in a sensitive part of his body, or that he needs to be compensated for missing out on the chance to gain stretch marks, experience morning sickness, or lose his ability to sleep on his stomach for months at a time.

Needless to say, even if you feel you must compensate the father for not experiencing the joy that is episiotomy by naming the children after him, it doesn't follow that it's traumatic for children to have a different last name from yours. As evidence, it's rare that people worry incessantly about the children having a last name different from that of a mother who remarries and changes her name a second time.

I DON'T LIKE MY LAST NAME ANYWAY

Less a pressure method than an excuse offered by women who caved to the pressure themselves but want to both retain their self-image as a never-bending antipatriarchal stalwart and also brush away doubts that their husbands who exerted pressure are anything less than completely feminist. Because this excuse seems airtight—if anything gives you an exemption from merely bending to patriarchal pressure, it's the idea that you are enamored of your husband's last name on its merits over yours—it has become wildly popular, to the point that it has lost any potential for believability. The statistical evidence at this point, if the people who use this excuse are to be believed, is that 99 percent of people with last names so horrible that the owner had to change them at the first chance just so happen to be female. This is a mind-boggling statistic that makes even less sense if you realize that the horrible last names that have to go are probably evenly distributed between men and women.

A likelier story is that women change their names under sexist pressure and then make up excuses afterward that make it easier for them not to be annoyed.

IT'S BETTER FOR EVERYONE IN THE FAMILY TO HAVE THE SAME LAST NAME

Close to "What about the kids?" but with more emphasis on the couple. In this case, the idea is that the only way that married couples can tell they're married is by having the same last name. The obvious question that this brings up is why, if married couples sharing a name is so damn important, it's all but forbidden to pressure men to change their names.

Or, if it's the groom making the case that you and he absolutely must share a last name, suggest that since he cares about this issue, then surely he will be eager to carry the burden of changing his last name. Enjoy the silence on the subject forever after this.

HYPHENATION IS STUPID

This assumes that you're going to hyphenate. If you won't hyphenate, good for you. Agree eagerly with the complainer that it's stupid and say that while you'd love to have the same last name as your husband, he was surprisingly less than eager to adopt yours. Since you didn't want to oppress him, you didn't push him to take your name and decided to drop the subject entirely.

YOUR LAST NAME IS ALREADY PATRIARCHAL

Most of us hail from less progressive backgrounds and wear our father's last name. And even if we do have our mother's last name, it was probably her father's. This argument assumes that if you're going to wear a man's last name, it should be your husband's. This argument assumes that only men can own names from birth, so while your husband's is his from birth, yours only belongs to your father.

But, even more annoyingly, this argument assumes that even if you assume both last names are patriarchal evils, you should choose the one that requires you to spend money and file paperwork. It's safe to say that anyone who thinks you should file paperwork with the government for no good reason whatsoever probably has a vendetta against you. Anyone who offers this argument, then, should be assumed to be out to get you, or at least make you fill out paperwork, and should be watched closely. He probably works for the IRS.

None of this means you're a bad person if you gave in to the pressure to change your name. It just means you're a dishonest person if you offer reasons other than, "The patriarchy is a mean, pressure-heavy asshole of a social structure, and this battle wasn't important enough to me to put up a fight." Some of us change our names, and some of us wear lipstick.

There Are No Good Options for Feminist Footwear: The Perils of Dressing While Feminist

In the ideal feminist world, one would be able to wave away the fact that a woman's footwear sets a standard by which to judge her character, but in a bizarre twist of fate, the choice of footwear can become even more important when a woman identifies as feminist. When a woman who doesn't call herself a feminist wears high heels or Birkenstocks, that's a measure of her individual character, but when a feminist makes a choice of footwear, she does so with the knowledge that her footwear will be held against her and every feminist everywhere. Rest assured, to make the entire task of determining the Proper Feminist Footwear even more fun, you can't win. Every shoe choice makes you a failure to feminism.

BIRKENSTOCKS

Comfortable and practical, but if you wear these shoes, you're upholding every stereotype imaginable about how feminists feel drawn to fashion choices that openly repulse sexual attractiveness. If Birkenstocks weren't objectively ugly, men could get away with them, and they can't.

HIGH HEELS

Bad feminist! Wearing footwear that fucks up your posture and your feet, that makes it hard to run or even walk, that marks you as decorative and otherwise useless, and all to fit into a beauty ideal that panders to male tastes, is nearly impossible to justify as "feminist" without resorting to thick academic language that mainly works by scaring people away from arguing.

STEEL-TOED DOC MARTENS

For two years in the '90s, the perfect footwear existed. Docs were tough. They didn't turn you into a decorative object. Yet you could get away with wearing them with sundresses if you wanted, which spared them from gaining a reputation as being the shoes of women who try to repulse sexual attention. They were perfect, so of course they had to go. Wear them now only if you want to be treated like a relic.

SNEAKERS

Don't you want to be taken seriously, as a woman? Sneakers with jeans, sure, and to work out, but if you are a Real Feminist, surely you have times when your footwear should speak to the serious woman who should be taken seriously. If you ever tried to pair sneakers with a suit—at least outside of doing so temporarily to make the walk to an office—you'd confirm all sorts of stereotypes about how women, and feminists especially, don't care to be taken seriously.

FLATS

The practical cousin of high heels. These suffer from the same prejudice as Birkenstocks in that they scream that the wearer is making a statement about how little she cares whether anyone thinks she's attractive. They're more subtle than flaunting armpit hair, but again, if you wear them, their ugly pragmatism will be held against all feminists because of your personal choice.

BARE FEET

Impractical outside of the house, and so invocative of a very unfeminist feeling of being strapped to the stove while pregnant. You can try to play off some of the seedier implications by going about in bare feet as evidence of your freedom-loving nature, but then you're emulating the irritating stereotype of the Kooky but Cute Girl, so familiar in movies made by guys reminiscing about their kooky fucks of old while married to commonsensical women now. Trying to live out that stereotype may up your number of casual sexual encounters by 5 percent, but it will come at the cost of looking like whatever the female version of a tool is. Plus, you encourage more sensible if mean-spirited people to stomp on your toes when you get in their way while dancing around all hippielike at rock concerts.

BALLET FLATS

Certainly sexier than regular man-stomper flats, but now you're back in Bad Feminist territory, prizing your cuteness over pragmatism. You can't walk very far in ballet flats without developing flat feet yourself. Still, they can't quite compete with high heels for marking you as a Bad Feminist, if only because you're unlikely to throw out your back walking around in ballet flats.

FLIP-FLOPS

The most undignified footwear of all time also doesn't pass the practicality test. For undetermined reasons, flip-flops have become the favored footwear of sorority girls nationwide, creating the bizarre sight on various college campuses of blonde girls with full faces of makeup and their hair done wearing sweatshirts, shorts, and flip-flops. It's a look that makes the viewer wonder how you can have the time to curl your hair and your eyelashes, but not find half a minute to bend over and tie your shoes. The impetus behind wearing flip-flops seems to be that they appear casual, but they also make it really hard to walk at more than a snail's pace, giving the wearer the proper feminine hobbled aura, presumably making her less threatening to men. Thus, they are the worst of all possible options, because you don't even get the sexy trade-off for the crippling downside.

DANSKO CLOGS

Evil shoes that seem to have been invented strictly to help feminists evade the "no good footwear" issue, Dansko clogs are comfortable without being ugly, fashionable without making you look like a slave to fashion. You can wear them with pretty much anything. Thankfully, they cost over $100 a pair, so a feminist sporting them can be called out for her classism. Also, they are most definitely not vegan-approved. As such, the perfect footwear for feminists still hasn't been found, keeping the equilibrium of the universe in balance, fueled by distressing guilt from well-meaning women facing down their closets every morning.

When Equality Means Men Get to Take Over the Kitchen Too

We still have never had a female president, and women make up but a tiny fraction of the number of CEOs of Fortune 500 companies, but this is still a "postfeminist" era, where equality has been achieved. That is, the only equality that counts in our unmentionably male-dominated area: is that men have finally been relieved of the great burden of being banished from certain areas that were traditionally the domain of women. One of the blessed areas that men have started to enter is the kitchen.

Naturally, the common feeling is that men are better at this than women, meaning that the postfeminist version of equality means that there are even more areas where women's talents can be degraded and denied. Not that this is any big surprise, of course. Even in the days when your average man couldn't even tell you where to find the sugar in his kitchen, people tended to carry on about how men cooking for paychecks were superior chefs to women cooking for their families.

In the pseudoequality era where men cook for their families, cooking has become the art du jour of the household. No longer are TV chefs relegated to the morning shows or PBS; now TV chefs have their very own network, and female TV chefs are subsequently required to be hotter than they were in the age of Julia Child. Rachael Ray even has done some pinup modeling. Fancy boutique grocery stores are popping up everywhere, and fancy boutique cookbooks are popping up on the shelves of bookstores. Clearly, it's not the worst trend in the world.

Except when women have to relinquish what was one of the few areas where we could lay claim to being excellent or even the very best at something. Or worse, when the sexist lording over women in the kitchen shades into emotional abuse. On Valentine's Day 2007, the *New York Times* ran a "lifestyle" story about women cowed into submission in the kitchen by their husbands who have to lord over one more area of life.

> *Yolanda Edwards was at a friend's house in Brooklyn for dinner when the hostess asked her to pull out a pot for boiling pasta. Ms. Edwards froze. As her friend looked at her in disbelief, she said she was not up to the job.*
> *"I used to think I was a good cook," said Ms. Edwards, an editor at the parenting magazine* Cookie. *"But my husband's a kitchen bully. He's so critical, I second-guess myself now."*

Her husband admitted that he felt that his wife was utterly incompetent in the kitchen, so he happily browbeat her until she was afraid that she would screw up boiling water. It makes you long for the days when such a man would put his feet up in the living room and send his wife scurrying to fetch him beer, but at least would give her the few square feet of the kitchen to herself.

There's not much you can do if you find yourself in the same unfortunate situation as Ms. Edwards. If you're married to a man who thinks equality means that he gets to feel he's better than you at absolutely everything, just demonstrate to him that you're perfectly competent at hiring a divorce lawyer. It's either that or one day you'll find that you're sitting quietly in the corner, trying not to breathe audibly for fear he'll yell at you for exhaling incorrectly.

If you find yourself with a friend married to such a kitchen dominator, though, you may have to face the fact that she's not facing up to her need to get a divorce lawyer straightaway. You may, however, be able to help her face up to the absurdities of the situation with a little old-fashioned passive aggression.

WHEN OVER AT THEIR HOUSE FOR DINNER, INSIST ON WATCHING TV WHILE HE BRINGS DINNER TO YOU

If he doesn't want to share the kitchen equally but instead rules over it like the housewives of old, he needs to buy into the whole package. If you're not willing to go that far, just ask him for a million favors while you're at the dinner table, so that he's so busy jumping up and down he can't eat a bite of dinner. My grandmother used to be so busy waiting on people that I don't think I ever saw her take a bite of food, at least inside her own house. Help your friend's maniacal husband see what that's like.

LURE YOUR FRIEND INTO A GAME OF CARDS AFTER DINNER, AND LET HER HUSBAND DO THE DISHES

Same theory. He who does not share the joy of cooking is not allowed to share the responsibility of cleanup.

IF ALL ELSE FAILS, PICK AT YOUR FOOD WHILE RHAPSODIZING ABOUT YOUR GIRLFRIEND'S COOKING FROM THE PAST

If he argues with you about how great her cooking was back when she was allowed to do it, smile indulgently and carry on as if you didn't hear him.

OFFER YOUR FRIEND A SAFE PLACE TO COOK

If your spare bedroom is open to friends who suffer from domestic abuse, then by god, your kitchen should be open to friends suffering from kitchen abuse. Often victims just need to be able to breathe a little, out from the barrage, to remember how good it felt. Declare a weekly girls' night and get her out of his kitchen and into yours. Watch some old episodes of Julia Child, make a mess in the kitchen, and drink cheap wine if you want to.

And look on the bright side: Not all men who venture into the kitchen plant a flag there and claim it in the name of the patriarchy. Some even pay their proper respects to the female forebears who forged some of the most beloved recipes, giving them credit for creative cookery even if those women kept their clothes firmly on and their images out of *Maxim*. Think of Michael Pollan writing eloquently in *The Omnivore's Dilemma* of the anonymous kitchenatrixes of yore, the ones who grew their own yeast and developed most of the world's various cuisines. We just need to make more like him, and peace will finally be declared in the kitchen.

The Bachelorette Party: A Lesson in Why Half-Assing Feminism Doesn't Work

The bachelorette party should be a win for feminism. Having a party for the bride that openly lays claim to the same rights to party, ogle, and generally act like an ass that men have claimed all along should be feminist in nature. Yet, if you've ever actually been to a bachelorette party, you can attest to the fact that somehow bachelorette parties fail to be feminist at all. In fact, they fail loudly and spectacularly. I leave it to the theorists to figure out why this is so (probably because there's no way to make a celebration of the patriarchal institution of marriage feminist), but mine is just to detail all the various ways that bachelorette parties fail in their feminist mission.

PHALLIC WORSHIP

Bachelor parties are about celebrating straight male sexuality at its sleaziest, so bachelorette parties should be about celebrating straight female sexuality at its sleaziest, at least in theory. In practice, bachelorette parties don't really celebrate female sexuality but instead celebrate the penis. At your ideal bachelorette party, penises should cover every available inch of space. There should be penis whistles, penis straws, plastic penises adorning the bride-to-be's trashy veil, and of course a penis-shaped cake. It's fun, sure, but it's regressive.

In other words, bachelorette parties are the epitome of postfeminism: By trying to lay claim to equality for women, we ended up participating in a bout of blatant phallic worship.

Men don't do this. Men don't have a vulva-shaped cake at bachelor parties, even though a bunch of men chowing down on vulva would be a much better visual pun than the penis cake. This is because while it seems initially insulting to chop up and consume the genitals of the opposite sex, it's actually symbolic worship. Men are not going to eat of the vulva like they were taking communion. And yet this sort of phallic communion is at the center of your average bachelorette party.

IT ENDS UP BEING ALL ABOUT THE MEN

Bachelor parties often center around getting men together to gawk at women, usually by paying those women at a strip club. And bachelorette parties center around gathering women around for men to gawk at. If you've ever been out and about with a bachelorette party, you'll know what I'm talking about; men seem to think that bachelorette parties are organized for the purpose of routing them drunk chicks who want to get naked.

If women could get some solidarity and not give in to the pressure to act like being a member of a bachelorette party means you are basically a free-roaming group of sex objects, then men would unlearn this assumption pretty quickly, but alas, there's always a handful of unreformed attention groupies in any bachelorette party. Men who follow bachelorette parties only need to see one pair of tits to reassure themselves they are correct in their assumption that bachelorette parties are all about routing naked tits to them.

IT'S NOT ENOUGH TO MAKE THE BRIDE MISERABLE— YOU HAVE TO HUMILIATE HER TOO

The dirty little secret about bachelor parties is that they're not supposed to be fun for the groom. The groom is supposed to bear witness to his single friends going on a bacchanalia that he can't really throw himself into wholeheartedly, unless he wants the wedding to get canceled when the bride catches wind of it. When you're a man, having your friends rub your nose in all the fun that you can't have anymore is considered punishment enough.

For women, however, it has to go a step further. I don't know if it's because people assume women don't resent giving up their freedom as much as men or if it's simply because women need an extra dose of punishment for presuming to have the same rights to a last bacchanalia before marriage, but that extra level of humiliation is there for brides-to-be. Part of the tradition is to parade her around in a veil, making a spectacle of her, and giving her tasks like ordering drinks with single-entendre names, all in an effort to make her feel really embarrassed to be getting married.

Granted, bachelor parties are beginning to pick up these humiliation rituals, too, so equality will be achieved in this area through regression, but that comes with the prewedding party territory.

THE WEIRD ASSUMPTION THAT THE BRIDE IS SEXUALLY NAIVE

Which really goes back to the penises everywhere. Why taunt a woman with many images of penises unless you're trying to hint that she's preparing for her first encounter with this particular organ?

THE STRIPPERS SUCK

Without bachelorette parties, the already meager opportunities for male strippers to dance in front of women would dry up completely. This is because male strippers are so singularly unentertaining that no woman in her right mind would look at them, except in a misguided attempt to create a postfeminist version of equal rights—in this case, the right to have naked people dance around in front of you prior to your wedding. To make the entire male stripper situation even more horrible, it's apparently mandatory for a number of women to scream and carry on, as if having a guy dressed like a firefighter wave his cock near your face were like winning the lottery. If you're so sexually deprived in your everyday life that seeing a guy get naked in front of you makes you squeal like a fourteen-year-old watching the Beatles in 1963, why on earth would you want to get married and make your deprivation permanent?

IT ENDS UP BEING ALL ABOUT MEN, PART TWO

A major feature of many bachelorette parties is the lingerie shower, which is similar to the bridal shower, but you buy lingerie instead of kitchen appliances. It's fun, no doubt, but there's something distinctly odd and patriarchal about buying gifts for your friend when you're really trying to buy them for her groom-to-be. If you've ever had the pleasure of buying a gift for a lingerie shower when you don't know the groom very well—or, sadly, even if you do, but in a strictly platonic way—you'll have the fun experience of standing inside a lingerie store, trying to figure out which frilly thing hanging on the racks will stiffen the penis of this guy whose tastes in that arena you don't know at all. At this point, I tend to long for the more traditional bridal shower, where you give the bride blenders and other things she wants for herself, because at least she isn't the proxy gift recipient. Plus, she can tell you what her kitchen needs the most without blushing up a storm about it.

Dodging the Bouquet Toss

O f all the sexist wedding traditions, this one might win for the most teeth-grindingly irritating. There's no way to win this one. If you're a lesbian, it's rubbing your face in the fact that you couldn't get married if you wanted to in most states. If you're single and straight and don't want to be married, just try to explain that one to your relatives. Single and open to marriage one day, and you are participating in a ritual that humiliates you by positing that you are so desperate for it, you're squealing and fighting other women for the mere hope. If you are married, you're cast in the role of standing around, smugly laughing at the single women clamoring to be you.

Attempts to make this ritual equal by having men fight for the bride's garter have failed miserably. Digging up five guys willing to give a half-assed show at barely reaching for the garter does not dish out the humiliation equal to flailing around with thirty women for a bunch of flowers you are then expected to hold up triumphantly. The only option is to boycott the bouquet toss. However, unless your friends or relatives getting married have an exquisite sense of humor, odds are you can't just say, while they are haranguing the single women to join in, "Sorry, but I've got a policy of avoiding any and all pressure to join this patriarchal institution of female servitude." If your friends and family do have that kind of humor, let me know. I want to be adopted.

Strategies for avoiding the bouquet toss that have worked for me a lot better than the favored one of joining in but not trying and looking vaguely disgusted:

OBVIOUS

Just have a sudden need to move your bowels when the bouquet toss is announced.

DUDE IT UP

Have the sudden urge to order an extremely masculine adult beverage during the bouquet toss. If you're in Fort Worth or Birmingham, a beer instead of a daiquiri will probably do you. If you live in a more cosmopolitan part of the country, you may have to Bond it up a bit and ask for a martini, shaken and not stirred. Scotch on the rocks works for all occasions if you can stomach it. The idea you want to convey is that you are too butch and bohemian for these girlie antics.

LUCK IS FOR PEOPLE WITHOUT MAD SKILLS

To make this strategy work, you have to find a man to flirt with long before the bouquet toss is announced. By the time the bouquet toss comes around, be so into flirting with him that none of these heterosexists will dare interrupt you. Why fuck up a woman chatting up a bona fide male human being, in order to make her squeal and run around with the hope of conjuring up a hypothetical one?

TOMBOYS DON'T GOT THE TIME

Ingratiate yourself with the DJ. Better yet, be the DJ. There is a force field that falls over the area behind the turntables/CD changer/laptop loaded with MP3s that will protect you from the patriarchy. However, it will not protect you from people making obnoxious requests for songs involving the word "Hammertime." Still a bit better than trying to look constipated when they announce the bouquet toss and then running off to the bathroom.

Coed Baby Showers, Single-Handedly Creating Antifeminists

Whenever some antifeminist guy is ranting at me about how men are the ones who are really oppressed because of the draft and all, I simply say to him that I'm happy to make women the only ones who sign up for selective service, if men will take on all the baby shower duties. Given the choice between the remote chance of being sent off to a foreign land to die and the immediate chance of being sent to an afternoon party where I have to suck down tasteless cookies and pretend that I think Snoopy-decorated onesies are the best thing I've ever seen, I'd gladly take the former. Of course, I don't speak for all women, especially not those who throw baby showers on a regular basis.

Still, times are a-changing. Women are signing up to be in the military, and the coed baby shower has come into being.

Being invited to your first coed baby shower will send you on an emotional roller-coaster with known stages, much like grief.

1. Elation. Finally, men are participating in baby showers!

2. Hope. Maybe this means that there'll be nachos and beer at the baby shower, instead of tasteless cookies and fruit punch! Maybe there won't be embarrassing party games involving taunting the mother-to-be over her giant belly. Maybe you'll even meet a single, progressive guy there.

3. **Dread.** What if it's not that way at all? What if the baby shower will be *even worse* with men there, because the women throwing it want to subtly punish men who get to have all the fun of making babies but none of the suffering, like labor, or baby showers?

4. **Dashed hopes.** You get to the party and find out that everything you dread is true, and that the single guys who are there are hiding in the bathroom.

5. **Resignation.** Well, the guys do need to share in the suffering of childbearing. The only question is, why do *you* have to go to the baby shower?

There's no doubt that people who throw coed baby showers are earnest and well-meaning. And they deserve our sympathies, since they're in a double bind. If you don't invite men to the baby shower, then you're being sexist. But if you change the party up to make it more appealing to the men you invite, you're implying that making the parties' fun is only to be done if men are invited.

Clearly, there's only one solution: Throw baby showers with nachos and beer, and don't invite men. Instead of party games where the guests have to place bets on how big the mother-to-be's stomach has grown, have a game where guests place bets on what sexual position she was in when she got pregnant. (Not advisable if she went to a sperm bank.) Instead of just getting the baby some gifts, chip in and get the mother something she'll need after the stress of having a new baby, such as a gift certificate for an hourlong massage.

Anything is better than the current situation at coed baby showers, with men standing around looking shocked at how tedious the entire thing is while women look humiliated at men discovering what passed for suitable entertainments for women in prefeminist days. But if you do find yourself at a coed baby shower, the best thing you can do is be grateful that no one has had the bright idea of inviting men to prewedding lingerie showers.

Fat Talk Roundtable

It's early morning and someone has brought donuts to work. Or it's midafternoon and there's a cake for someone's birthday. Regardless of the exact justifications, the formula is always the same. Women plus fattening sweets equals the ritualistic roundtable of self-flagellation.

"Oh, I shouldn't!"

"And I've been so good today!"

"My butt's gotten big enough, but . . ."

And then it's your turn. On one hand, you know that fat is a feminist issue. You know that these rituals are just the sort of thing that upholds the patriarchy and reinscribes the idea that women's main role in life is to be decorative sex objects.

On the other hand, you don't want the reputation as the stuck-up bitch at the office, the one everyone gossips about because she thinks she's such hot shit. Granted, you're an intelligent person, and you might be very good at rationalizing away this fear. You might tell yourself that you really want to participate in the rounds of self-disparagement because it's a female bonding ritual. You're doing it for the sisterhood. But underneath it all, it's that fear of having everyone look at you with sparks of resentment in their eyes.

So you reach for the donut and say, "I really shouldn't, but I guess the diet can start tomorrow. Ha! Ha!"

These little failures to stand up for your feminist principles are nothing to be ashamed of. What else are you going to do? Stand up on the table and lecture everyone about pushing back against the patriarchy? Are you going to turn to Cindy from Accounting and say, "Cindy, you are more than your ass! You are a good accountant, a faithful wife, and you tell some pretty funny jokes!"

Or maybe you could shove the box of donuts to the floor and beseech everyone to quit talking about the food as a source of individual failure and start talking about our collective responsibility for healthier food and sustainable agriculture. That should go over well and not confuse anyone at all.

Passive aggression won't work too well, either, not if you're trying to avoid having all your coworkers hate you. Meekly piping up, "Do we have to do the rounds of self-hate talk?" will only induce your coworkers to peg you as the tedious goody two-shoes. If you're sincere about wanting people to stop with the self-hate talk, it won't do to make the self-hate talk seem like a gloriously un-PC form of rebellion against prigs like yourself.

The only real solution is to pretend you're diabetic. This works best if you start at the beginning of your employment at a place and maintain the facade carefully. No snatching candy off your coworkers' desks. No happy-hour girly drinks. If you're willing to go the distance, you may have to avoid big bowls of pasta for lunch as well. You probably won't have to go so far as to fake blood tests on yourself, especially if you act private about it, but still, it's a lot of work. Might be worth it to avoid the "I'm so fat" roundtable of predonut penance, though.

The downside to this is that all the avoiding of sweets and carbs at work might make you lose a lot of weight, which becomes another occasion for people to challenge your feminism inadvertently. "How do you stay so skinny?" is a question that can't be shrugged off without running the same risk of becoming the official office stuck-up bitch.

Part 8.

RESOURCES:
HAVING FUN
WHILE SURVIVING

PC Feminist
Insults Do Exist

For those of us who are old-fashioned, politically correct, feminist sorts who still get a huge kick out of insulting people we dislike—and there are more of us than you would think out there—the perennial problem is coming up with nasty names to call people that are not sexist, racist, or classist. This is harder than you would think. Even "asshole" is considered by some to be homophobic or sexist. But never fear: A scientific study involving a pitcher of beer and a rowdy willingness to fight it out determined that there are a handful of already existing curse words that are completely PC-feminist. The big one was "tool," which not only can mean "tool of the patriarchy," but is in fact used in such a way. All the evidence you need is this: When you're looking at Adam Carolla and trying to think of what to call him, what's the first word that comes to mind if not "tool"?

The word "douchebag" as a feminist-approved insult was more contentious. There are some who say that such an insult falls under the general umbrella of "insults insinuating that women are nasty." But there are those of us who say that bags of douche are the very definition of tools of the patriarchy. Everyone knows the *Our Bodies, Ourselves* mantra about how douches are nothing but tools to teach us that women are nasty and need to have our insides scrubbed out with battery acid to be considered acceptable, at least in between bouts of washing clothes that smell of the wholesome earthiness of the American male. The debate seemed at a stalemate, with one side saying "douchebag" was the equivalent of calling someone a "pussy" and the other side saying that it works more as a synonym of "tool." So, I made a chart demonstrating that "douchebag" has roughly the same meaning as "tool" and not "pussy," to show that calling someone a bag of a bona fide tool of the patriarchy is indeed a Feminist-Approved insult.

In general, adding "-bag" to the end of words is an efficient way to insult someone without getting into the social-hierarchical danger zone. The rule of thumb is to take a bag and fill it with something unpleasant, mentally speaking, and ascribe that to the person you're talking about. "Assbag" is okay, but some would probably stand up for the pleasant nature of asses, though it's safe to say that "unwashed assbag" would be universally deemed unpleasant. "Shitbag" is indefensible as a pleasant thing that shouldn't be used as an insult. "Bag o' Christian wingnuts" could be the worst thing you could call someone, outside of "pedophilebag."

ANNOYING MAN	TOOL?	PUSSY?	DOUCHEBAG?
Adam Carolla	Yes	No	Yes
Rush Limbaugh	Yes	No, but he is a wiener	Yes
The "Can you hear me now?" Guy	I hate to say it, but no	Yes	No, because if he's a douchebag, then we are all douchebags
Emeril Lagasse	No way	Probably	Of course not, though he is irritating
John Tesh	Yes	Yes	Yes
Ted Nugent	YES	No, though it would be cool if he were	Yes
Tony Snow	Yes	No	He seems too unnatural to be called anything as squishy as a douchebag, so one point against my argument.
Fred Durst	Yes	No, but he is a jack-off	When he cries, his eyes lose that not-so-fresh-feeling for a reason.

Not Your Mama's Chick Flick

Hollywood is the home base for pushing tired gender stereotyping, churning out movie after movie where women function mostly as ornaments, sex objects, nurturers with no internal life worth noting, or MacGuffins for the real heroes—the men—to fight over. To add insult to injury, the supposedly female-friendly response is the creation of a genre commonly known as "chick flicks," where women actually have starring roles—as bubbleheads who live primarily to please men and be cute girlfriends with a few charming but harmless character flaws. That said, there are some movies out there, even if they're few and far between, that actively resist the patriarchy or subvert the usual typecasting of half the human race. Here are some of my favorites, though as usual this list is far from exhaustive:

28 DAYS LATER

The zombie movie that spanned a thousand arguments about what's scarier—fast or slow zombies—didn't receive much ink spillage for its indictment of patriarchal violence. Too bad, because while the chair-clutching horror of the movie makes it fun, the satire of a masculinized violent culture is what makes the movie stick with you. Right off the bat, the introduction of Selena, a hardass who teaches the hero Jim the basics of surviving, lets the viewer know that this horror movie isn't playing by the usual rules. But things kick into high gear when Selena and Jim have to fight off a group of soldiers who've convinced themselves, quite wrongly, that the survival of the human race requires controlling and abusing women. Attention to craft-loving viewers: Sewing features big in saving the heroes from annihilation.

GIRLS TOWN

A tad dated, but still worth watching. A group of high school girls avenge their deceased friend after finding out that her suicide was related to a rape. A walk through the early '90s, from the presence of Lili Taylor to a soundtrack featuring artists from Queen Latifah to Luscious Jackson. It's a definite icon of the "gritty realism" phase of independent filmmaking, of which Spike Lee's *Do the Right Thing* reigns supreme.

ROSEMARY'S BABY

The famous '60s film about devil spawn reads well as a feminist fairy tale warning of the dangers that await the woman who trusts in the patriarchy. At every turn in Rosemary's tragic tale, a little resistance against patriarchal dominance would have served her well, but her unwillingness to buck expectations placed on her as a young wife leads to the tragic end, when she becomes the unwitting mother of the Antichrist. The horror in the movie springs from the helplessness of a pregnant woman at the hands of a community that treats her body like public property, not only forcing her to bear the child but also meddling relentlessly with her prenatal care, trying to separate her from her friends, and just generally acting like pregnant women are stupid cows with the mental abilities of children. Recommended viewing for Mother's Day. That a rapist like Roman Polanski can produce a feminist masterpiece is just more evidence that ours is an inconsistent world.

THE STEPFORD WIVES

Based on a novel by Ira Levin, the man who also wrote *Rosemary's Baby*, this horror/sci-fi movie is probably the most explicit and over-the-top film about the dreaded patriarchy, verging on genuine paranoia. The twenty-first-century attempt to remake this film about men who turn women into sex-and-housecleaning robots failed miserably, since it turns out you can't make a movie where sexism is the source of horror while also promoting sexism. Stick to the '70s version, even though the idea that men idealize wives who wear big dresses and straw hats still makes not a whit of sense.

THELMA AND LOUISE

No feminist film list would be complete without the legendary film, starring Susan Sarandon and Geena Davis, that features two women going apeshit on asshole males after killing a would-be rapist. Good acting, good action, and Brad Pitt naked—in a fair world, this is what people would mean when they said "chick flick."

FAST TIMES AT RIDGEMONT HIGH

Most high school comedies treat girls like exasperating obstacles between the male heroes and access to the tits and ass. Not so with this classic '80s comedy, which doesn't romanticize high school from the point of view of a middle-aged man, but shows it as it is in all its cringeworthy, immature nonglory. Jennifer Jason Leigh's character, Stacy, lives out the all-too-common story of the girl who has sex out of obligation instead of desire and ends up in an abortion clinic for her trouble. Unlike most movies that have storylines like this, however, there's no overwrought moralizing or puffed-up judgment of Stacy, just the sense that she learned a little something and went on to have a life that worked out just fine.

Also, it's funny. Between the actual humor and the intelligent view of sexual/romantic relationships, it's hard to believe that this movie was written by the same man who wrote and directed the train wreck *Jerry Maguire*.

THE APARTMENT

One of my all-time favorite movies, so I have to make a feminist case for it, even though it's focused around a male protagonist and the main female character attempts suicide because her older, married lover won't divorce his wife and marry her. That said, this movie touches on a theme dear to many feminist hearts, which is the way our dog-eat-dog world puts people in situations where they feel they have to sell their souls to get ahead. Jack Lemmon's character, Bud Baxter, routinely compromises his basic morals and dignity to kiss ass at work and get promoted, only to find out that getting ahead in the corporate economy may not be worth the loss of self-respect required.

But that's not why I think this is a feminist movie. What's appealing on a feminist level is the character Fran, played by Shirley MacLaine. Fran could have been written as a traditional female victim, but instead, she's one of the more multifaceted love interests ever to grace to silver screen. Fran's unfortunate problems, from her crappy job to her crappy boyfriend to her suicidal depression, are all firmly portrayed as assaults from the outside world on her otherwise strong, witty personality. Fran's overall awesomeness is irrelevant in the capitalist patriarchy she dwells in; she's been pegged as a working-class woman and has no access to any avenue outside that. Few movies then or now are as willing to offer an unflinching portrayal of the lack of choices for working-class women.

ALIEN

Most horror movies that reduce the cast to the Last Girl Standing present that girl as a fragile virgin who can scream a lot, but *Alien* doesn't condescend to the survivor in this way. By moving the setting from a suburban neighborhood or the backwoods of Texas to outer space and making the monster a little bit closer to a literal rapist (a walking, fanged penis that impregnates its often male victims), Ridley Scott was able to free his movie from some of the tedious restrictions and make horror-movie survivorship live up to its feminist potential. Sigourney Weaver's character, Ripley, moves further and further away from the victim role and becomes darker over the various sequels, but the original is still far and away the best of the bunch.

MURIEL'S WEDDING

Another two-women-against-the-world road trip movie, but without all the Sturm und Drang of *Thelma and Louise*. Muriel is a victim of patriarchal romanticizing of weddings and marriage, and she just knows she'll have a big wedding one day and be vindicated as a woman who has a right to exist. In her quest to find a man, she instead finds an old friend, Rhonda, who's more interested in finding one's self through dancing to ABBA and having a generally good time than languishing in hopes of finding a man. The movie sends up the wedding–industrial complex in part, but it's also a brutal denunciation of the way that women stab each other in the back to win the Best Girl award in a male-dominated culture. It'll make you squirm, but it's generally pretty funny, and the themes of the movie are basically never explored in the Hollywood machine.

REAL WOMEN HAVE CURVES

It's not surprising that feminist themes pop up more in indie films, but luckily, the star America Ferrara moved on to the big leagues and carried that feminist sensibility with her to her show *Ugly Betty*. The main character, Ana, is struggling between two choices: moving out into the larger world and getting a college education, or following her mother's plan for her to stay at home and pursue a more traditional female life. Along the way, Ana falls in love, of course, but the movie pointedly avoids making her boyfriend her identity, and even shows them parting ways happily as Ana moves on to follow her dreams.

Tuning in the
Feminist TV Set

TV Land seems to be a patriarchal wasteland most of the time. Between the endless stream of sitcoms positing either that Father Knows Best or that Father Knows Nothing but at Least Is Fun While Mother Is a Skinny but Annoying Prig—and the also endless stream of crime shows, where the camera slowly lingers over the alluring figure of the pasty-white but still sexy rape and murder victim—it sometimes seems that a feminist can't catch a break. It's not that you want all your TV shows to be political treatises—far from it. But it would be nice to be entertained by shows that didn't make you roll your eyes every two minutes at the tedious sexism.

There's some relief, if you know where to turn the dial. Some of these shows are over and done with, but thanks to the magic of DVD, they are one Netflix rental away from warming your boob tube.

BUFFY THE VAMPIRE SLAYER

You know it's on the list, so it might as well be at the top. The show hit all the right notes from the beginning, with the main character being very capable at her line of work, yet very human and still painfully concerned about having some sort of feminine identity. It was a hit with feminist-minded types, because the stories always hinged on this very real struggle between the sense that women can be respected for their actual capabilities and the hard reality that they aren't. Buffy's dual life as a vampire slayer at night and a normal girl by day reflected back to the audience their sense that their talents and intelligence weren't being perceived correctly by the larger world, largely due to sexism.

Plus, it has old-fashioned mean vampires who bite and kill and need to be killed. Also, the dialogue is about five steps above most television in quality—snappy, funny, bright.

FIREFLY

Sadly, this show lasted less than a season, but it was so popular with fans that it eventually turned into the movie *Serenity*. Luckily, you can get the entire series on DVD. It was created by the same man who created *Buffy*, Joss Whedon, and it has the same snappy dialogue and interesting plot twists that make *Buffy* so entertaining. *Firefly* is a combination of a Western and a sci-fi show, following a bunch of renegades running from an oppressive government and making money on the side as petty thieves.

What makes the show interesting from a feminist perspective is that it features Whedon's strong desire to subvert typical gender roles. A Western has to have a prostitute, of course, but in the futuristic world of *Firefly*, whores are finally paid the handsome salary they deserve, and their sexual skills are highly respected. The ship's engineer is a mechanical genius and rather free with her affections, and she never gets punished for her promiscuity, which alone rates the show as feminist. The ship's lieutenant is both a stone-cold warrior and possibly the only genuinely happily married major female character on TV in a decade, and the off-the-charts-genius fighting-machine character is also female. At every turn in the show, women's equality is taken for granted, which would make the viewer wonder what took so long, if she weren't huffing popcorn and wondering what's going to happen next.

UGLY BETTY

A show about a supposedly ugly girl dropped into the middle of the high-fashion magazine world doesn't sound like it's got a lot of feminist appeal, but it does. If nothing else, the show rates high for subtly critiquing the idea that there could be such a thing as a truly feminist fashion magazine, by having the so-called powerful woman leader of this magazine demonstrate that she's just as much a shallow backbiter as anyone else in the fashion publishing industry. The starvation diet and general phoniness of the fashion industry is endlessly lampooned. The sister on the show is a good mother without being perfect. Betty is shown to be a sexual being without having to be a fashion model herself to earn it. The father is shown as someone who thrives on domestic work like cooking, and there's no indication that he should earn some sort of special accolades for this. Homosexuality is vigorously defended on the show as part of a healthily diverse environment. All told, it's an intriguingly profeminist show, with just enough soap opera to it to keep you waiting impatiently for the next installment.

THE GOLDEN GIRLS

The rule is in turns called the Bechdel Test or the Mo Movie Measure, after the comic strip artist Alison Bechdel and her most famous comic creation. The idea is that a movie's baseline measure to get it past the teeth-grindingly sexist phase is to have two female characters who have at least one conversation with each other that's not about men. *The Golden Girls* isn't a movie, but it passes the Mo Movie Measure with flying colors. The characters on the show talk about men to each other, sure, but they talk about everything else under the sun. And it's funny and well-acted. Despite the fact that each character is a broadly drawn type on the page, on the show, they are surprisingly well-rounded. It helps that there aren't many stereotypes of how old women are supposed to be outside of the Cat Lady or the Bitter Crone, neither of who are on this show.

The Golden Girls was later remade to be more appealing to men, as *Sex and the City*. Making the women younger and richer didn't do much to build the male audience, but it did make some cash for HBO. Now it's assumed that a show with four female leads has to be built around the concept of sex, but as *The Golden Girls* showed, it could be built around being retired with almost as much sex and twice as much snickering.

MAUDE

Before she was on *The Golden Girls,* Bea Arthur was a loudmouthed asshole of a feminist on *Maude.* She was initially meant to be the overtly feminist version of her cousin Archie Bunker on *All in the Family,* but it became clear over the course of the show that her attitude problems came from a very different place, making her a more sympathetic character. Watching old episodes of *Maude,* which is now out on DVD, is both entertaining and educational. A lot of the struggles of the old women's liberation movement have been forgotten to time, since the feminists won so decisively, but those struggles are preserved on *Maude.* For instance, I didn't know that men didn't generally wear wedding rings until the '60s, until I saw an episode where Maude fights her husband Walter over his refusal to wear one.

The show is also famous because Maude was the first TV character to choose to abort a pregnancy, and nothing bad happens to her because of it. Sadly, she was probably also the last for a long time to have a realistic experience with abortion.

BATTLESTAR GALACTICA

The new version of the old TV show takes place in a world where human-created robots named Cylons have rebelled against their creators and dumped nuclear bombs all over the twelve planets colonized by humans, killing all but fifty thousand of them. The survivors are on the run, in a fleet of ships that are all passenger ships except the *Galactica,* which is the military headquarters.

Starting from that premise, the creators have imagined a human civilization where women's equality is a given. The president of what's left of humanity is a woman, as is the top fighter pilot on the *Galactica.* The show also subtly skewers the patriarchal elements of our culture, especially with regard to the way the Cylons have a shallow, patriarchal, monotheistic religion. Humans, however, worship multiple gods, and their favorites are Athena and Artemis.

The show receives raves from critics because of the stellar acting and the morally complex story lines that draw heavily from current American politics. Some of the portrayals of feminist issues are muddied and complex, but that realistic touch is what makes it interesting, despite the fantastical premise.

onsider this just a sampling of female-led and feminist-friendly music that I personally enjoy. It's not comprehensive or even close to it, but it's a good place from which to start digging around for feminist-minded music in an era when misogyny tends to sell more records. It's also to show that there's a lot more out there than chicks-with-acoustic-guitars in terms of feminist music, if you're willing to look for it. If you like an artist and want to hear more music like hers, a good place to start is by checking out the websites of the record labels she publishes on, especially if they're indie labels. Most labels have a specialization, and if you like one of the bands, you'll probably like others.

LE TIGRE

The royalty. Kathleen Hanna's adventure into lo-fi dance pop turned out to be as brilliant a manuever as starting her riot grrrl punk band Bikini Kill, except even more so. Groovy, funny, and unabashedly pro-feminist and pro-gay, their albums are a must-have for any feminist. Of particular note is the song "Viz," where Le Tigre member JD Samson sings enticingly of the simple joy of butch lesbian visibility.

SLEATER-KINNEY

The riot grrrl movement demanded that the punk and indie rock establishment quit ignoring the fact that women can play too. Sleater-Kinney made it impossible to ignore the message. For a time, they were a shot of life into a dead rock scene, bringing up the possibility that a group could be loud and entrancing without having the traditional guitar/bass/drums setup. But more than that, the combination of Carrie Brownstein's banshee wail, Corin Tucker's sometimes harmonizing, sometimes contrasting vocals, and both women's ever-insistent guitars left a huge impression on the listener. Nearly out of the blue, this aggressively feminist, all-woman trio became the best band in rock music for a time, which had the nifty side effect of stomping out the idea that female musicians were just window dressing or tokens.

BRATMOBILE

One of the top old-school riot grrrl bands, famous in no small part for their cover of the Runaways' "Cherry Bomb." But check out their original music: chirpy, poppy girl punk that sneaks the feminist message in like a Rohypnol in a beer. You'll be singing along to tunes like "Punk Rock Dream Come True" before you realize that it's consciousness-raising about domestic violence.

SHONEN KNIFE

Japanese punk trio that somehow makes bubblegum punk sound like kicking ass. If you're feeling impotent with anger about sexism in general, watch their video for the song "Banana Chips," in which their impossibly cute cartoon selves peel and slice bananas in such vivid detail that it becomes a single entendre. It's so over-the-top that it's impossible to be impotently angry for long.

DUSTY SPRINGFIELD

One of the icons of '60s R&B was a cantankerous lesbian from England, which goes a long way toward showing what was cool about the '60s. Springfield heard the R&B coming over from America and knew she had to imitate that sound. She was so stubborn about getting the sound exactly as she had it in her head that she quickly gained a reputation with producers and engineers for being something of a bitch. Looking back, they probably were just unused to women speaking their minds—and being right.

LADY SOVEREIGN

Spastic rapper from England who wears her crudeness as a badge of honor. She routinely dares people to guess if she gives a crap if they think she's a brat or hate her for her hairiness or general unladylike behavior. (Hint: She doesn't.) How can you not love someone who spits in time to the beat?

AU PAIRS

Don't let the music snobs fool you; men didn't utterly dominate the postpunk era. While everyone is running to reclaim Gang of Four, the real gem of the era is the Au Pairs. Lead singer Lesley Woods was riot grrrl before riot grrrl, an open lesbian feminist who wrote smart, self-righteous, funny lyrics mocking everything from monogamy to the complaint that men and women are so equal . . . just different. Their music holds up incredibly well after all this time, and their Peel sessions are particularly noteworthy.

BEASTIE BOYS

Hard to believe the group that had a song about girls doing your dishes on their first album would become adamantly pro-feminist, but they did. I saw them in high school and was really impressed by a flier they handed out before the show that chastised male audience members who harassed or groped women in the pit. The flier said that women and girls were there to dance to the music and enjoy the show just like the men. Sure, it seems like a basic concept to an educated feminist, but to a sixteen-year-old girl, the very idea that male musicians could stand up for me and mine was a revelation.

BIKINI KILL

The original riot grrrl band, screaming loud punk rock with a dark sense of humor. Only Kathleen Hanna can take lyrics like "I'm a self-fulfilling porno queen" and make them sound both angry and amused all at once. The song "Rebel Girl" is a classic call to arms for third-wave revolt. While Hanna doesn't like being called a leader, she is indisputably an icon of feminism to the generation that thoroughly mixes their pop culture and their politics.

MISSY ELLIOTT

Cool rapper who makes cutting through the sexist bullshit and rising to the top of the charts look easy. Don't let her fool you; it's not. Herky-jerky hiphop that sounds remarkably smooth, all because Missy's voice will lull you with her flow. Some people say, "What Would Joan Jett Do?" and I add Missy Elliott to the list of people to emulate.

X-RAY SPEX

Snotty teenage punk band from 1970s Britain. They only really lasted one album because the two female members got into a fight, under the misimpression that a band couldn't really have more than one female member. Forgive them their youth and inability to see they weren't beholden to sexist paradigms, since they were otherwise willing to blow right through them. The music and lyrics anticipated riot grrrl twenty years ahead of time, with lead singer Poly Styrene screaming, "Up yours!" to the very concept of bondage while winking at the erotic possibilities of it. The song "Germ Free Adolescents" retains its status as a uniquely fascinating rock-song take on the modern hygiene neuroses, hinting at the sex-phobia and body hatred issues that would escalate in the coming decades.

Plus, they have a saxophonist who actually rocks and started another band called Essential Logic, well worth checking out.

THE GOSSIP

Beth Ditto, the lead singer of the Gossip, is cool distilled. A big fan of outrageous fashion and makeup, she's renowned for her bold stage act, which often includes stripping down to her underwear—damn the opinions of the fainthearted people who suddenly grow concerned about your health if you're fat and undressed in front of them. The band hails from Portland now, but Beth and the guitarist, Nathan, grew up in Searcy, Arkansas. Beth's earthy, dramatic singing style shows her Southern roots, right up to the Pentecostal influence, but instead of singing lyrics about Jesus or men who done wrong, she sings odes to the gay rights movement and songs advising her listeners to avoid no-'count friends.

Their sound started out as bluesy-punk, but when they replaced their original drummer with Hannah Blilie, their sound took a turn toward disco punk. Beth's big voice suits her new role as a disco diva, and their music tends to turn even the most sullen crowd of hipsters into dancing fools.

LADYTRON

Mostly included for the name, because I like ladies. The band is two men and two women, with the women up front, but the semi-ironic name that pokes fun at the way female singers get all the focus is a good indicator of the pleasures of this band's electropop. It's reminiscent of the good side of new wave in the early '80s—the wry, intelligent New Order–style new wave, instead of the cheesy Culture Club version.

Plus, they put out a mix disc of their favorite influences called *Softcore Jukebox*, where I learned exactly how kick-ass '60s garage band Shocking Blue really is and how fun cheesy pop like Cristina can be dropped into a mix at just the right time.

PRINCE

Despite the unfortunate lingerie routine in "Purple Rain," Prince has actually been quietly feminist for his entire career. Given his choice of equals to work with, he generally chooses to promote women's careers. I'm not sure why he does this, but the most logical explanation is that he knows talented women often have a lot fewer choices, and he's trying to equal it out some. And yes, while he's famously slept with some of his protégés, by no means is this his regular habit. In fact, some of his most famous protégés are the backbone musicians for the Revolution, the famous couple Wendy Melovin and Lisa Coleman. His long-standing professional relationships and mentorships with female and openly feminist musicians include Sinead O'Connor, Kate Bush, Rosie Gaines, Sheena Easton, Sheila E., the Bangles, Ani DiFranco, Chaka Khan, Cyndi Lauper, and his longtime bassist Rhonda Smith. You could have guessed it from his playfully sexy music, but it's nice to have it confirmed that the Purple One holds the opposite sex in high esteem.

SONIC YOUTH

Like the Au Pairs, Sonic Youth was feminist before feminist was cool. They are well-known for their hypnotic guitar sounds that fade into loud punk rock, but their clever lyrics are often well worth giving a listen. The song "Swimsuit Issue," on their album *Dirty,* was the first song I'd ever heard address sexual harassment and objectification, and needless to say, the drippingly sarcastic tone of bassist Kim Gordon's singing helped shape my image that feminists were really cool, drippingly sarcastic hipsters. For better or worse, I've since found out that feminists are diverse, but I've tried to live up to the image since then, on principle.

THE SLITS

Seventies British punk band that learned to play from the Clash and later toured with them. The Slits were remarkable for many reasons, not least their name and their rather spastic reggae-influenced sound that manages to be infectious. Lead singer Ari-Up joined when she was just fourteen, and her brazen, off-kilter singing draws your attention and makes you want to sing along, even though that task proves difficult, since it's nearly impossible to figure out what she's saying. Ari later took her big pipes across the Atlantic to become a dancehall singer.

Reading biographies of the band, it's hard not to conclude that they had no idea how their streetwise, cheeky, feminist-sounding lyrics would hit people's hot buttons. Unfortunately, they learned the hard way when Ari was assaulted while walking down the street by a knife-wielding man mumbling something about slits. Still, she recovered, and those lyrics, when you can understand them, give a devious sort of feminist pleasure, such as, "Typical girls buy magazines / Typical girls feel like hell / Typical girls worry about spots, fat, and natural smells."

TRIBE 8

Lynnee Breedlove and his band Tribe 8 took the idea of take-no-prisoners lesbian rock to a whole new level. Not content to rest on the laurels of having a metal-friendly hard rock sound with giggle-worthy lyrics, the band also put on a hell of a live show, with Breedlove often performing topless with a strap-on hanging out of his pants, a strap-on he'd often invite straight boys in the audience to suck. (And good sports often did.) But even if you never got a chance to see them live, their albums are good fun if you're into ass-crackingly loud hardcore punk rock.

THE RAINCOATS

Another late-'70s English punk band, but even more experimental with their sound than most. They excel at jerky, unpredictable songs with intriguing vocal harmonies and a noisy, Velvet Underground–esque backdrop of screeching violin. Their lyrics set the gold standard of good-humored feminism, from the song "Fairytale in the Supermarket" to their cover of the Kinks' "Lola," where they sing as women singing as a male narrator who falls for a woman who turns out to be a man. And it's all very catchy, as that level of queering up the rock canon should be.

THE BUTCHIES

From the pun-happy title of their album *Are We Not Femme?* (a play on Devo's first album title, *Q: Are We Not Men? A: We Are Devo!*) to their cheerfully poppy punk tunes, the Butchies are the queercore band to throw on the player when you want to get happy. They have the perfect late-'90s pop punk sound, with a feminist-lesbian bent to their lyrics.

THE BLOW

This band out of Portland, Oregon, consisting of Khaela Maricich (and formerly, her friend Jona Bechtolt), makes the sort of lo-fi dance-pop rock that became popular after Le Tigre blew the doors off and made it cool again. The Blow excels at the very hard task of making lo-fi pop invigorating; as the early MTV era showed us, it's far too easy to let the synthetic sound take over and drain all the organic fun out of music. The Blow never lets that happen. It's a perfect example of a band that's taken off in no small part because of the twenty-first-century indie rock world's attempts at overcoming sexism; the Blow has talent and does well, and no one makes an issue out of how Maricich is, gasp, a woman.

CRASS

British punks in the '70s had a startlingly pro-feminist bent, it seems. This band, who titled an album *Penis Envy*, might take the gold ring in the category. Their music is tumultuous and interesting, and definitely for ears a bit more accustomed to avant-garde rock, which is unsurprising, since the band sprang from an art collective.

WANDA JACKSON

Most people remember '50s rockabilly as being a male-only endeavor, but in truth, one of the shining lights of the genre was a woman. Jackson started off as a country and western singer but made the move to rockabilly at the urging of friends who saw her potential. Jackson never made it as big in rock music as someone like Elvis Presley or Buddy Holly, but she still had a couple of minor and memorable hits with songs like "Let's Have a Party" and "Fujiyama Mama." Her career as a rock musician compels one of the big what-ifs in rock history—in this case, "What if Jackson hadn't had to work in such a sexist culture?" The idea of a female rock singer made a lot of people anxious, and that—coupled with Jackson's immodest love of loud colors, big earrings, and makeup—made her a frequent target of antirock critics. She eventually returned to singing country and western music, but her big voice and infectious guitar make her rockabilly records a treat to this day.

L7

I'd love them just for their name, which references a '50s beatnik play on calling someone a "square." The band came of age in the fabulous riot grrrl era of the '90s, but like the Lunachicks, they had a harder, more heavy-metal edge to their music. The band also founded the Rock for Choice movement in 1991, using punk rock to educate fans about reproductive rights and raise money for activism. The combination of a lunkhead-friendly, heavy-metal sound and fiercely feminist politics made this band a lightning rod for a lot of the hostility coming from the subset of men who'd prefer to keep rock music a penis owners–only club. (Ones made out of silicone don't count.)

Things came to a head in 1992, when the audience abuse of the band came to head, and in retaliation against audience members who were throwing things at her, lead singer Donita Sparks threw misogynist fear back in their faces by pulling out her tampon and hurling it into the audience. When I saw them a year later in concert at the tender age of sixteen, I was sort of hoping Sparks would do it again, but the show was relatively tame—except for the music, of course.

Feminist Blogs: When You're Ready to Quit Dabbling and Proceed to Heavy Feminist Use

Feminist blogging is both exciting and dangerous stuff. Exciting because no matter where you live or whom you have to tolerate in your real-life world, you can find like-minded feminists online for all your issue-hashing, patriarchy-blaming, and bitching needs. (We even engage in old-fashioned leftist infighting, in case that part of being an activist is important to you.) Blogs are somewhat hard to write about in print form, because new ones emerge and old ones die every day. Still, if you want to immerse yourself in the feminist blogosphere, it's wise to get a lay of the land. Here are some of the most important blogs to check out, though please take my assurances that this is only the tip of the iceberg in terms of all the great feminist writing out there:

PANDAGON

www.pandagon.net

Mine. 'Nuff said.

Okay, more to be said: Jesse Taylor started this blog and asked me to join him after a few years of running it. We blogged together about every issue under the sun, including feminism, until he had to quit in order to work in the real world, leaving management to me. I promptly added an all-star cast of feminist-friendly liberal bloggers. You get to learn what Pandagon means after becoming a familiar face in the comment threads.

FEMINISTE

http://feministe.us/blog

Started by Lauren Bruce and currently run by Jill Filipovic, with her co-blogger Piny, Feministe has always been a heady combination of cheekiness and in-depth analysis of issues from a feminist perspective. As Jill is a lawyerly sort, this is a good blog to hit up for some legal perspectives on feminist issues. Feministe has one of the best comment sections on the Internet, in my never-humble opinion. Its threads often run into the hundreds of comments without getting stupid—rare feat in the blogging world.

FEMINISTING

www.feministing.com

Another group blog with a large number of bloggers. Jessica Valenti started the blog with the intention of giving young feminists an Internet home, and she has succeeded with another always-interesting commenting community. Where *Jane* failed to be *Sassy* all grown up, Feministing has succeeded. Feministing positions itself as a catchall news source for feminists; it specializes in short, frequent posts covering a range of topics important to young feminists every day. It tends, therefore, to be more comprehensive in its coverage than most blogs, and it has plenty of interesting features, such as video blogging and regular interviews with activists.

ALAS, A BLOG

www.amptoons.com/blog

In one of the great ironies of feminist blogging, the first big feminist blog with a rowdy commenting community was run by a man. The cartoonist Barry Deutsch didn't quite expect his blog to become the most prominent feminist blog on the Internet, but when events overtook him, he stepped up to the plate and became instrumental in helping support emerging feminist bloggers in creating the feminist blogosphere. With its rotating cast of guest bloggers, Alas always makes for interesting reading.

ECHIDNE OF THE SNAKES

www.echidneofthesnakes.blogspot.com

Economist J. Goodrich started this blog, under the persona of an angry goddess after having had quite enough of conservative politics. Behind this persona of a vengeful snake goddess, Echidne has managed to carve out a reputation as one of the more calm, polite feminist bloggers, always willing to take the time to carefully dismantle antifeminist arguments through the deadly venom of statistics and airtight reasoning.

FAUX REAL

www.fauxrealtho.com

Lauren Bruce returned to blogging after retiring from Feministe and added some more music snobbery and ruminations on pop culture to her usual plateful of intelligent feminist commentary.

PAM'S HOUSE BLEND

www.pamshouseblend.com

Pam Spaulding co-blogs with me at Pandagon but also runs one of the best feminist/gay rights blogs at Pam's House Blend. Pam not only provides first-rate coverage of LGBT issues, but she also wades into the fight with the fundamentalist right, providing endless amounts of coverage pointing to the depths of crazy they will reach.

I BLAME THE PATRIARCHY

http://blog.iblamethepatriarchy.com

Twisty Faster, the spinster aunt and radical feminist from Austin who writes IBTP, is one of the most consistently engaging and funny writers on the Internet. That said, her blog isn't for everyone, as she'll tell you up front, but intended for an audience of "advanced patriarchy-blamers." Twisty holds forth in her ever-funny way on the subjects of pornification, women who equate being a better sex object with "empowerment," and the grave importance of regular taco consumption in the fully realized life.

WOMEN OF COLOR BLOG

www.brownfemipower.com

Brownfemipower updates her blog frequently on a dizzying array of topics generated from her interest in examining the intersections between racism and sexism. From covering the teachers' union riots in Mexico, to blogging in support of the struggle for the Palestinian state, to her own strong protests of racism within the American feminist movement, Brownfemipower leaves no stone unturned in articulating her vision for a broader international movement for social justice.

BITCH PH.D.

www.bitchphd.blogspot.com

Dr. B, as she's affectionately known in the feminist blogosphere, started her charmingly named blog as a minor space to bitch about life and sexism while she scaled the ladder of academia in her real life. She ended up writing an interesting mix of casual feminism, discussions of parenting her young son, and the trials and tribulations of living in an open marriage. In the process, she built up a vigorous, diverse commenting community that's willing to talk about feminism, parenting, and sex with a frank attitude.

HOYDEN ABOUT TOWN

http://viv.id.au/blog

Founder tigtog describes a "hoyden" as a "woman of saucy, boisterous or carefree behavior" and decorates her revolving banner with various examples, from Emma Peel to Katharine Hepburn. She and her co-blogger Lauredhel write about feminist politics from an Australian perspective and with the courage of their convictions. Their willingness to speak their minds, even if it offends some people (including this feminist at times), makes their blog an always thought-provoking stop on the Internet.

A FEMINISM 101 BLOG

http://finallyfeminism101.wordpress.com

This is where various feminist writings are catalogued so that people with questions about feminism have a basic resource. It's a popular website toward which to redirect anyone who aggressively asserts that because of a misquote they've read from Andrea Dworkin someplace, all feminists think sex is rape.

SHAKESVILLE

www.shakesville.com

Melissa McEwan named her blog Shakespeare's Sister (shakespearessister.blogspot .com) after her online handle, which in turn was inspired by a Smiths song. Then she started adding co-bloggers, one after another, until she realized that her large cast of writers made hers an official group blog, so she changed the name and URL to Shakesville. The blog has the rowdy feel of a noisy party where all the guests have sparkling wits—overwhelming at times, but not to be missed. They're fiercely feminist and pro-gay, but the blog extends beyond political discussions and has a good mix of talk about life, entertainment, and nostalgia.

Full disclosure: Melissa McEwan is my fallen comrade-in-arms. We worked on the John Edwards campaign together and together we were attacked in the media by professional right-wing noise-generator Bill Donohue of the Catholic League until we resigned from the campaign. Melissa, true to blogging form, has not allowed this misfortune to diminish her voice but has grown stronger and angrier because of it.

KINDLY PÓG MO THÓIN

http://kindlypogmothoin.com

"Póg mo thóin" is Gaelic for "kiss my ass," a sentiment which fits the blogger Zuzu well. Zuzu started out as a popular commenter on various feminist blogs, known and liked for her acerbic wit and low tolerance for fools. Her popularity propelled her to a spot as a blogger on Feministe, where her inability to brook bullshit won her a few enemies but many friends. She eventually moved on to run Kindly Póg Mo Thóin solo. There she blogs about everything from body-image issues to single life in New York City.

PUNKASSBLOG

http://punkassblog.com

I'm biased in favor of this blog, since it was founded by my consort and fellow cat custodian, but I'd be remiss if I didn't mention this stellar feminist blog with a bad attitude. Punkass Marc founded the blog and added the ever-witty Kyso Kisaen, the ever-brilliant Sabotabby, and the ever-irascible Junk Science to the fold. The blog is a hodgepodge of feminist contempt for sexist pop culture, love of science and environmentalism, and the all-too-rare mature attitudes about international politics.

ANGRY BLACK BITCH

http://angryblackbitch.blogspot.com

Activist and crack-up Shark-Fu describes her own blog as a place for "practicing the art of bitchitude." In her sporadic but amusing prose, Shark-Fu takes on the antiwoman, racist nonsense of the mainstream media and the right wing with a tone that never leaves you in doubt that the relentless drumbeat of bullshit in the world continues to baffle as well as irritate her.

LAWYERS, GUNS AND MONEY

http://lefarkins.blogspot.com

The title of this blog, taken from a Warren Zevon song, misleads a number of early readers into thinking this is yet another blog run by lawyers talking about the law. In reality, it was founded by three political science academics to talk about politics—a distinction that ends up being more minor than you'd think. Still, feeling which way the winds blew on this, they added an actual feminist lawyer named bean to the crew, along with a more mysterious blogger who just goes by the name of d. Even before the addition of bean, however, LGM was integrated into the feminist blogosphere because of blogger Scott Lemieux's sharp political analysis on women's rights and reproductive justice. Scott's willingness to go to the mat against male pundits who shove women's issues into a ghetto has earned the blog an esteemed spot in the eyes of feminist blogging fans.

MAJIKTHISE

www.majikthise.typepad.com

Pronounced, believe it or not, "magic thighs." The blogger Lindsay Beyerstein named the blog after a philosopher character from the Hitchhiker's Guide to the Galaxy series, because her blog was initially about philosophy with some politics mixed in. Eventually, the politics took over, and Lindsay started on a career as a freelance journalist. With her philosophical training in hand, Lindsay approaches the issues of the day, including the feminist ones, with a firm rationality and a willingness to get embroiled in even some of the nastiest controversies.

OUR BODIES, OUR BLOG

www.ourbodiesourblog.org

Christine Cupaiuolo used to run the blog for Ms. but left after an overhaul in management. Now she blogs at Our Bodies, Our Blog, which is affiliated with the book *Our Bodies, Ourselves*. Most of her blogging is link and news roundups, always with an eye toward expanding understanding of women's heath issues and, a dose of Christine's sense of humor.

WIMN'S VOICES

www.wimnonline.org/WIMNsVoicesBlog/

The blog arm of Women in News and Media. WIMN's Voices is very heavy on guest blogging, which means that there's a steady diversity of women's voices on various issues relating to the portrayal of women in the media and the continuing problem of women being unrepresented in the news media.

PINKO FEMINIST HELLCAT

http://pinkofeministhellcat.typepad.com

The blogger Sheelzebub writes at Pandagon now as well, but I started reading her snappy, angry feminist blogging long before that. Sheelzebub slices through antifeminists, racists, and apologists for general obnoxiousness like she's cutting butter. Her blog became well known for her solid coverage of rape cases, and for her ongoing satire of the fascist leanings of the crazy 25 percent of our country in her President-for-Life series.

THE SIDESHOW

http://sideshow.me.uk

Avedon Carol wants it known that her name is indeed Avedon Carol, not Avedon, Carol. One of the pro-sex feminists with battle scars from the '80s porn wars, Avedon has gone on to be an all-around lefty political blogger who still dives into feminist defenses of porn, erotica, and left-libertarian attitudes on sex and drugs in general. She's such a prolific writer and thinker that she mostly uses her blog to record various "you should be reading" links, always with smart, feminist commentary and occasional pictures of pretty bras she likes, to liven things up.

REAPPROPRIATE

www.reappropriate.com

Jenn writes about fighting sexism and racism from the perspective of an Asian American woman, and her writing is always good food for thought. She has a strong ability to write about some of the conflicts between antiracist thought and feminist thought without causing hurt feelings, except in those who deserve their feelings hurt. I doubt she's as unflappable as she seems, but I appreciate her strong, steady voice in a discussion in an intersection of politics where things can get heated quickly.

Selected Titles From Seal Press

For more than thirty years, Seal Press has published groundbreaking books.
By women. For women. Visit our website at www.sealpress.com.
Check out our blog at www.sealpress.com/blog

30 Second Seduction: How Advertisers Lure Women Through Flattery, Flirtation, and Manipulation by Andrea Gardner. $ 14.95, 1-58005-212-6. Marketplace reporter Andrea Gardner focuses on the many ways that advertising targets women and how those ads affect decisions, purchases, and everyday life.

The Bigger, The Better, The Tighter the Sweater edited by Samantha Schoech and Lisa Taggart. $14.95, 1-58005-210-X. A refreshingly honest and funny collection of essays on how women view their bodies.

She's Such a Geek: Women Write About Science, Technology, and Other Nerdy Stuff edited by Annalee Newitz and Charlie Anders. $14.95, 1-58005-190-1. From comic books and gaming to science fiction and blogging, nerdy women have their say in this witty collection that takes on the "boys only" clubs and celebrates a woman's geek spirit.

Chick Flick Road Kill: A Behind the Scenes Odyssey into Movie-Made America by Alicia Rebensdorf. $15.95, 1-58005-194-4. A twentysomething's love-hate relationship with picture-perfect Hollywood sends her on a road trip in search of a more real America.

We Don't Need Another Wave: Dispatches from the Next Generation of Feminists edited by Melody Berger. $15.95, 1-58005-182-0. In the tradition of Listen Up, the under-thirty generation of young feminists speaks out.

Naked on the Internet by Audacia Ray. $15.95, 1-58005-209-2. A sex rights advocate reveals that many young women use the internet to explore their desire and develop their sexual identities.